The Airman's War: World War II in the Sky
Overlord: D-Day and the Invasion of Europe
Victory in the Pacific
The Sea Rovers: Pirates, Privateers, and Buccaneers
War Clouds in the West: Indians and Cavalrymen, 1860–1890

War Clouds
in the West

Albert Marrin

WAR CLOUDS IN THE WEST

Indians & Cavalrymen
1860-1890

Atheneum · New York · 1984

Library of Congress Cataloging in Publication Data

Marrin, Albert.
War clouds in the West.

Bibliography: p. 213
Includes index.
SUMMARY: Narrates the late nineteenth-century
struggles of the Native Americans to survive against
the increasing flow of white settlers moving west
and taking over the land.
1. Indians of North America—Wars—1866–1895—
Juvenile literature. 2. Indians of North America—
Wars—1862–1865—Juvenile literature. 3. Indians
of North America—West (U.S.)—Wars—Juvenile literature.
[1. Indians of North America—West (U.S.)—Wars] I. Title.
E83.866.M35 1984   973.8   84-4621
ISBN 0-689-31066-8

Copyright © 1984 by Albert Marrin
All rights reserved
Published simultaneously in Canada by
McClelland & Stewart, Ltd.
Composition by Maryland Lino, Baltimore, Maryland
Printed and bound
by Fairfield Graphics, Fairfield, Pennsylvania
Designed by Mary Ahern
First Edition

To
the peaceful folk,
who tried to find a better
way

Contents

We took away their country and their means of support, broke up their mode of living, their habits of life, introduced disease and decay among them. And it was for this and against this that they made war. Could anyone expect less?

—General Philip Sheridan, 1878.

Prelude

July 17, 1859. It is a sparkling summer afternoon with a soft breeze blowing across the Wyoming prairie.

Thirty ox-drawn wagons lumber along, their canvas covers billowing like puffs of cloud against the blue sky. They are moving northward on the Oregon Trail, bound for South Pass through the Rocky Mountains and the rich country of Oregon and California beyond. Their journey, which began with bugle calls at Independence, Missouri, in May, will end with prayers within sight of the Pacific Ocean sometime around Thanksgiving.

The settlers call their wagons "prairie schooners," because they resemble sailing vessels underway on a calm sea. But instead of salt water, their element is grass—a rolling sea of green grass. The grassy sea stretches to the horizon, unbroken in every direction. The breeze passes over it, rustles it, making it sway in long, graceful swells.

The air, though dry, is heavy with the sweet scent of grass mixed with the not-so-sweet odors of sweat and fresh manure. All is quiet, hushed, except for the wagon train's own sounds. A driver snaps his whip to remind the oxen to keep moving. Tin pots and pans, hastily packed by tired youngsters, rattle and clang. Wheels creak rhythmically save for the thumpety, bump, bumping each time they roll over prairie dog holes. A lone eagle circles high above, its keen eyes following the activity below.

3

Indians watch a wagon train crossing the Bozeman Trail through the Rocky Mountains.

Someone points to a dust cloud rising in the west. Beneath it, moving swiftly on horseback, are men with brownish skin and hair of the blackest black. Almost naked, they wear only a narrow strip of cloth around the waist and moccasins of soft deerskin on their feet. Colorful markings cover their faces and bodies. The Cheyenne are coming.

The wagon train jolts into action as drivers lash their oxen, drawing blood. They know it is foolish to form a wagon circle, since they'd make perfect targets standing still in the open. Within minutes the long line is arranged in two parallel columns. Every man that can be spared leaps to the ground with his rifle to form a circle around the wagon train; armed women crouch in the rear of each wagon. The settlers will fight and march at the same time, the wagons advancing behind a screen of riflemen.

The Indians also have a plan. They will not charge into the defenders' line of fire, but sweep around them in single file, forming a circle of their own.

It is a strange scene, viewed from above. Two circles, one inside the other, are moving in two directions at once. Everything becomes a blur of movement and noise. Gunshots rattle from the inner circle. Each settler goes down on one knee, aims, fires, reloads, and continues walking until ready to fire again. The Cheyennes reply with swarms of arrows and some shots, since few have guns.

The attack ends within half an hour. The Indians, satisfied with running off a few horses, ride away with whoops of victory. No one on either side has been killed or seriously hurt.

There was nothing special about this fight—except for those who took part in it. There had been fights like it before and there would be fights like it again. For these fights were part of a larger struggle in which the Indians of the far West would lose their homes and find themselves unwanted, strangers in their own land.

Two ways of living and looking at the world struggled against one another. Crazy Horse, war chief of the Oglala Sioux, spoke for all Indians when he said: "We did not ask you white men to come here. The Great Spirit gave us this country as a home. You had yours. We did not interfere with you. The Great Spirit gave us plenty of land to live on, and buffalo, deer, antelope and other game. But you have come here. You are taking my land from me. You are killing off our game, so it is hard for us to live. Now, you tell us to work for a living, but the Great Spirit did not make us to work, but to live by hunting. You white men can work if you want to. We do not interfere with you. And again you say, why do you not become civilized? We do not want your civilization! We would live as our fathers did, and their fathers before them."

one

The Buffalo Hunters

The struggle between Indians and whites began when the first white people landed along the Atlantic coast. As their numbers grew, they spread out in search of fresh lands to clear for farms and settlements. And wherever they went, they found the land already occupied.

The Indians may have been America's first inhabitants, but the whites believed they had a better right to the land. The average United States citizen thought of himself as "civilized" and the Indian as a "savage." Where whites worshipped one God, the Indians prayed to the forces of nature. Whites had science and machinery to help with their work, while Indians lacked even iron and the wheel.

Many whites saw nothing wrong with tricking such backward people into selling their lands cheaply, or with their government's refusing to honor its promises to them. The United States Government made hundreds of Indian treaties and broke them all.

Where treatymaking failed, there was always force. Tribes that stood in the path of the whites' advance were defeated one after another. Sometimes they were conquered not in open battle but in ways that we today think of as dishonorable. Indians were given "gifts" of blankets from people who had died of smallpox. Whole tribes, such as the Mohegans, were almost wiped out by this highly contageous disease.

By the 1850s the frontier had reached the line formed by the Mississippi and Missouri Rivers. Beyond, to the West, lay the Great Plains of North America. Eleven major tribes inhabited the Plains: Assiniboin, Arapaho, Blackfoot, Cheyenne, Comanche, Crow, Gros Ventre, Kiowa, Kiowa-Apache, Sarsi, Sioux. Among these were some of the most warlike peoples the Americans had ever met. To understand their struggle, we must first understand their way of life.

The Great Plains reach southward from Canada to the Mexican border and westward from the Mississippi River to the Rocky Mountains—one third of the United States. The plains are not pancake-flat, but curve gently with the curvature of the earth. Except for clumps of cottonwoods growing along the riverbanks, they are treeless, covered only by grass.

The rivers have given the plains their few higher places. During millions of years rivers dug wide, deep valleys. Rain and wind then cut into the valley walls to form steep-sided hills called bluffs; bluffs that stand alone on the plains are known as buttes.

Although the plains climate is mild and dry most of the year, there are times when it is very unpleasant. Summers can be blistering hot, with the temperature soaring to over one hundred degrees in parts of Texas. Plains winters would please polar bears. Arctic winds from Canada send the temperature to fifty degrees below zero. Mountainous snow drifts make it impossible for people or large animals to get around. Cattle, and people, have frozen solid when trapped in sudden blizzards. The plains also receive their share of cloudbursts, tornadoes, and hailstones as large as golf balls.

This area once teemed with wildlife. Antelope, elk, and deer roamed in vast herds, fearing only the gray wolf and coyote; the grizzly bear feared no creature. Prairie dogs lived in underground colonies in tens of thousands; one scientist figured that Texas alone had eight hundred million of these squirrel-like creatures. But the true king of the plains was the buffalo. Resembling oversized cattle, these creatures may have numbered as many as forty million.

Life was harsh for the Plains Indians, but also satisfying and rewarding. Everyone knew their place, knew who they were and where they belonged. They knew what to expect from their tribe and family, and what these expected from them in return. Indians had no doubts about what career to follow or the path to be taken in life.

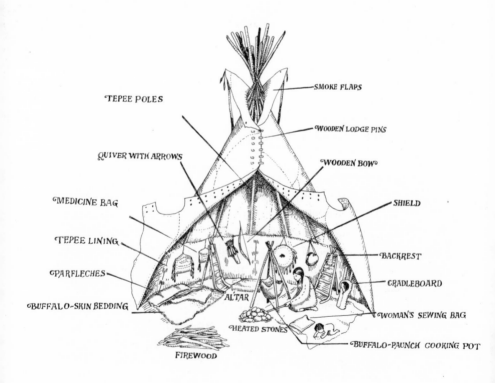

The horse made it possible for the Plains Indians to follow close behind the buffalo herds upon which they lived. Whenever it was decided to move, the women did all the packing, loading, and unpacking. The wooden cage at the back of the travois kept young children from falling off the platform.

Daily tasks were strictly divided between the sexes. Men hunted, raided, and made war. Women did the heavy physical work that kept the home together. They chopped firewood, carried water, cooked food, and made the clothing and household goods, including the house—the tipi. This tent of buffalo hides was warm in winter and cool in summer, the perfect house for people who had to break camp in a hurry.

As soon as the camp criers gave the signal, the women took down the tipis and packed them with the family's other belongings on a platform fastened between poles. Before the Plains Indians had horses, these platforms, or travois, were

9

pulled by dogs. If there weren't enough dogs, the extra bundles went on the woman's back, together with any child too small to walk. Arriving at the new campsite after an all-day march, she unpacked, set up the tipi, and prepared the evening meal.

Every girl dreamed of marrying in her teens. She had been taught from childhood that being a wife and mother was the only way to live. A young man attracted a girl's attention by tugging at her robe or whistling softly as she passed. At night he stood behind her father's tipi to serenade her (and the neighbors) with love songs played on a flute.

Indian camps were crowded places that offered little privacy. If a girl was interested in a boy, she came out of the tipi with a blanket over her shoulders. The boy stood in front of her and she opened the blanket, covering them both. Villagers went about their business, pretending not to notice. Kid brothers and sisters stood by, giggling and puzzled at the strange doings. Meanwhile the couple put their cheeks together and whispered into each other's ears. A pretty girl might have three or four suitors standing in line nearby, each waiting his turn in the blanket.

Marriages were arranged not by young people, but by their elders. A girl didn't even have to know her future husband. It was only important that he had seen her, or heard of her, and wanted her for his bride. One day his parents arrived at the entrance to her father's tipi with gifts. These weren't for the girl, but for her family as a sign of respect. Although the girl could refuse a marriage offer, she usually accepted her parents' decision. The wedding followed a day or two later. Her father brought her to her groom and, after more gift-giving, this time to the bride, they became husband and wife.

In time, the wife became a mother. A child's birth was cause for celebration throughout the camp. The father and grandfathers lit bonfires, invited everyone to a feast, and boasted about the healthy, handsome child.

The Plains Indians were kindly parents who knew how to make their children feel wanted and loved. Besides its own parents, the child was surrounded by caring adults. Grandparents, uncles, aunts, cousins, and family friends were always nearby to keep a watchful eye. They openly showed their love by constantly patting, hugging, and speaking affectionately to children.

Even the youngest children had a lot of freedom. They were free to crawl about, to explore, to get hurt—and to learn from their adventures. Yet one freedom, which white children have always had, was forbidden on the Great Plains. The child had no freedom to *cry*. Enemies might be nearby, and a crying infant might give away a camp's location. The moment an infant began to cry, it was picked up, rocked, cuddled, and fed. A grandmother might cry along with it, to "help." If this didn't work, the wailing baby was taken with its cradle-board and hung on a bush outside the camp until it cried itself out. After a while it forgot about crying.

Indian parents were strong-willed people who knew what they wanted from their children. Children were asked, never told, what to do and how to behave. Moral teaching began early. The youngster was expected to be respectful to the elderly, honest, and generous to the poor.

Of course children, being children, broke the rules. When they did, their parents never shouted at them, much less spanked or slapped them in the face; a slap was a terrible insult that had to be avenged. A misbehaving youngster was reasoned with until it saw its mistake. If reason failed, it was embarrassed in front of the whole community. Such treatment usually didn't have to be repeated.

Plains Indian children knew nothing of the whites' book-learning. A girl learned everything she needed from her mother and women relatives. A boy's schoolroom was the Great Plains itself. His lessons were based on nature, which he had to master in order to survive.

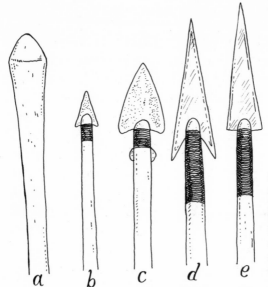

Different types of arrowheads were used for different purposes: a. blunt head for stunning not killing; b. small flint point for hunting birds; c. flint points used in war; d & e. steel warheads bought from white traders.

a *b* *c* *d* *e*

War clubs had stone heads or were tipped with sharp pieces of flint. Some even had iron nails or old knife blades.

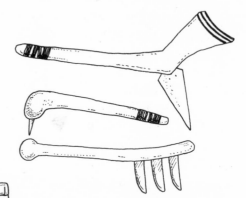

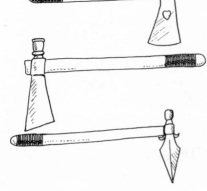

The word tomahawk means "cutting tool." Indians made their own tomahawks with stone heads, but preferred the iron heads sold by whites. A tomahawk could be used as an axe for chopping or as a throwing weapon. The one in the center has a pipe bowl on top and might be used for ceremonial purposes.

Although the Plains Indians gathered wild fruits and vegetables, their main food was meat. A boy grew up knowing that one day he would have to kill, and go on killing for the rest of his life. At the same time he was taught never to kill carelessly or for "fun." The Indian was no sportsman. He believed that life was sacred, a gift from Wakan Taka, the Great Spirit, alive equally in the sun's rays and in the tiniest creature.

The Indian killed solemnly, with regrets and prayers. The youngster learned always to beg an animal's forgiveness for taking its life and to explain that he needed it for food. And, having killed, he should not be wasteful. It was sinful to throw away anything that could be eaten.

An Indian boy trained to be a hunter as an athlete trains for the Olympic Games—hard and all the time. Boys of nine or ten learned to go without food for days and to stay awake and alert through the night. Rolling in the snow and diving into icy streams prepared them for tracking game in the winter. Quick reflexes were developed by chasing butterflies and catching them in flight. The youngster then rubbed the wings on his chest to "borrow" the insect's grace and speed. Boys in their early teens ran for hours without stopping to rest or take a drink. By the time they were fourteen, their bodies were tough as wire and flexible as rubber. Weak, sickly youngsters died early.

A boy learned to hunt as soon as he could walk and hold a weapon. His father or uncle gave him a knife and a scaled-down set of bow and arrows. Hundreds of hours were spent teaching him to track game, until he was expert at shooting the smallest bird off a distant bush.

The Indian boy studied plains wildlife with no equipment but his senses, his intelligence, and his curiosity. He put his ear to the ground to locate the larger animals, as well as people on horseback, by their vibrations. His sense of smell was almost as keen as the wolf's. He could tell from miles away if a fire was natural or man-made and who made it, Indians or whites. He could touch an animal's droppings and tell by shape, hardness and warmth the kind of animal it was, what it had eaten, and if it was nearby.

Above all, the Indian boy used his eyes. One rule was drummed into his head until it became second nature: Look closely at anything and be patient. A boy would go alone to the top of a butte and sit motionless, observing the animals and their ways. He learned that sand thrown up in piles meant that young deer had been playing. Lots of shallow tracks close together told him that deer were grazing and moving along slowly. A wolf's off-key howling, or many magpies screeching at once, meant that something important was happening and that he'd better be careful.

Religion was as important a part of Plains Indian life as learning hunting skills. Indians believed that everything in nature was actually two things at once. It was a physical thing that could be seen and touched, and an invisible, spiritual thing. If you knew how, you could see the spirits, learn from them, and win their friendship. Every famous warrior and hunter had a special spirit-helper to protect him and give him success.

Indian boys (but not girls) were taught about the spirits and prepared to see them when the time came. At the age of fourteen, the youngster hiked alone to the top of a distant butte. The boy neither ate nor drank anything for four days and nights, but stayed awake, begging Wakan Taka to send him a vision.

If he was lucky, an animal spirit visited him. It could be the spirit of any creature from the puny gnat to the lumbering buffalo or the slithering snake. The spirit taught him to make a medicine bundle, his personal package of special objects—odd-shaped stones, animal teeth, feathers, tobacco—that would give him magical powers. The spirit might also tell him the secret meaning of certain signs and sounds. For example, a bird-spirit once told a hunter to listen to the birds before starting out. If they sang in a high pitch, he'd have a good day; if not, he'd better stay home for his life was in danger.

Visions were real to the Indian in the same way as something we want very much is real when we see it in a dream. We'll never know what would have happened had the hunter disobeyed the bird-spirit's warning. What we do know is that the Indian's faith in spirit-helpers often gave them the added confidence to succeed at something that was especially difficult or dangerous.

A boy became a man when he killed his first buffalo. The buffalo, or American bison, ruled the plains. It roamed in vast herds that spread as far as the eye could see. When the buffalo stampeded, as they often did during lightning storms, the earth trembled as during an earthquake.

An adult buffalo bull stood seven feet tall at the shoulders. It was nearly twelve feet long and weighed a ton. Although it had poor eyesight, it could sniff out an enemy a mile away if the wind was right.

Then look out! An angry buffalo was a terrifying sight. Head down, horns pointed forward, it pawed the ground. Its bloodshot eyes glowed like red coals. Hot breath steamed out of its nostrils. The buffalo was so strong that it often kept charging when it should have fallen dead. Buffalo have run half a mile with a bullet hole in the heart large enough to put a finger through.

Indians said that everything they needed for a good life, except drinking water and wood for tipi poles, came from this generous animal. Buffalo skin made wonderful leather, strong and long-lasting. Rawhide was skin that had been cleaned and dried in the sun. When applied wet and allowed to dry in place, rawhide cords could fasten most things and keep them

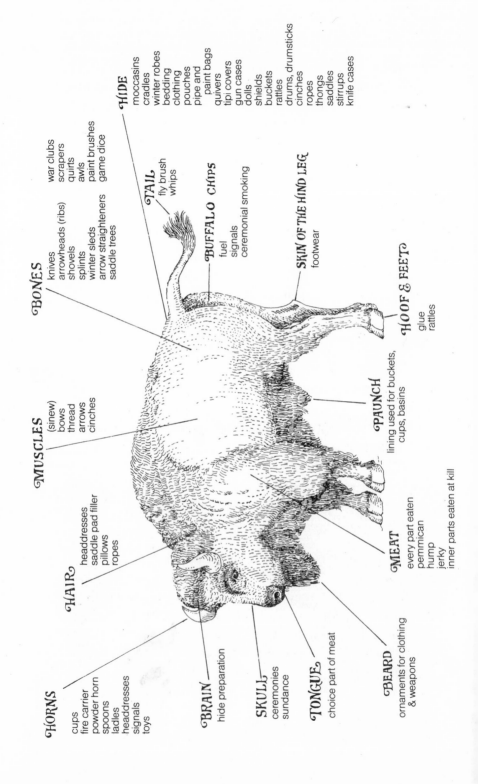

HIDE
moccasins
cradles
winter robes
bedding
clothing
pouches
pipe and
paint bags
quivers
tipi covers
gun cases
dolls
shields
buckets
rattles
drums, drumsticks
cinches
ropes
thongs
saddles
stirrups
knife cases

BONES
knives
arrowheads (ribs)
shovels
splints
winter sleds
arrow straighteners
saddle trees

war clubs
scrapers
quirts
awls
paint brushes
game dice

TAIL
fly brush
whips

BUFFALO CHIPS
fuel
signals
ceremonial smoking

SKIN OF THE HIND LEG
footwear

HOOF & FEET
glue
rattles

MUSCLES
(sinew)
bows
thread
arrows
cinches

PAUNCH
lining used for buckets,
cups, basins

HAIR
headdresses
saddle pad filler
pillows
ropes

MEAT
every part eaten
pemmican
hump
jerky
inner parts eaten at kill

HORNS
cups
fire carrier
powder horn
spoons
ladles
headdresses
signals
toys

BRAIN
hide preparation

SKULL
ceremonies
sundance

TONGUE
choice part of meat

BEARD
ornaments for clothing
& weapons

fastened forever. The finer skins were tanned and used for everything from blankets to tipi covers. Tanning was woman's work, as much a source of pride to her as a hunter's skills. A skin was stretched on the ground and kept in place with

Cheyenne women begin to tan buffalo skins by pegging them out on the ground to dry. A mixture of buffalo brains and other waste meat was later added to tan the skins.

wooden pegs. After scraping away the fat and muscle, the woman applied a paste made by boiling buffalo brains, fat, and bone marrow. A few days later the skin was washed and pulled over a sharp-edged board to make it soft.

Buffalo hair was woven into rope and stuffed into gloves and moccasins for warmth. Tails became fly whisks. Horns made handy drinking cups and storage jars. Hoofs were boiled for glue. Ribs formed runners for sleds. Skins were sewn together, blown up, and used as "buffalo boats" to cross rivers. Sinew, a fiber from the tendon that runs along the animal's backbone, made strong thread and bow string. Thin bones could be shaped into knife blades and awls to punch holes in leather.

Even the buffalo's dung served the Plains Indians. "Buffalo chips" were lumps of digested grass that littered the ground. When it rained, these chips stayed dry at the center, making a hot, nearly smokeless fire to warm a tipi or cook a meal.

Buffalo meat was a wholesome diet rich in nearly every nutrient needed by humans. The best parts were the tongue and flesh from the hump, which were cooked. The buffalo even provided the cooking pot. The paunch, or inner lining of its stomach, was tough and leathery. The Indians suspended it from poles, placed meat, vegetables and water inside, and added heated rocks to bring the stew to a boil. When the paunch-pot became soggy after a few days, it was also eaten.

Not all buffalo meat was cooked. Blood was drunk warm from the animal's veins. The liver and kidneys were eaten raw. The intestines were swallowed whole, without chewing, like thick strands of spaghetti.

The Indians put aside large amounts of meat for the winter, when snow and cold made it difficult to move around. Meat could be preserved either as jerky or pemmican. Jerky is any meat that is cut into long, thin strips and hung up on

Cheyenne women use stones to pound wild cherries, pits and all, into a paste that will be mixed with buffalo meat and fat to make pemmican. Pemmican was a perfectly balanced diet and one of the Indians' favorite foods.

racks to dry in the sun. Jerked buffalo could be eaten raw or cooked in the regular way.

Pemmican was a delicacy. Women used stone-headed hammers to pound strips of jerky into fine shreds. Dried berries were pounded into the meat, seeds and all. Finally melted fat was poured over the mixture, forming cakes that were stored in rawhide cases called parfleches. Pemmican could keep for three or four years, a tasty, high-energy food valued even by white frontiersmen.

The main buffalo hunt took place in late summer, when the grass was thickest and the animals at their fattest. Before setting out, some tribes performed the Sun Dance, the Plains Indians' most sacred religious ceremony. A tall, straight cottonwood with a forked top was cut down and placed in the center of a circular enclosure built of brushwood. Volunteers, the tribe's bravest young men, stepped forward. They had prepared for the ordeal by going without food and sleep for four days. Everyone watched as the medicine men (priests) cut two sets of parallel slits in each side of their chests. Skewers of smooth wood were then passed under the skin between each pair of slits. Cords were tied from the corners of each skewer to the fork of the Sun Dance pole. As the drums throbbed, each man chanted "Wakan Taka, be merciful to me that my people may live. It is for this that I am sacrificing myself."

The dancers stared wide-eyed at the sun. Although the pain was terrible, they leaned back and began to pull against the cords. An hour passed. Two hours. Three hours. Blood ran down their chests and legs, forming puddles on the ground. One by one the skewers tore through the skin until all the dancers were free. They were happy, though hurting, because the buffalo hunt could now begin.

Each tribe was divided into smaller bands, which set out separately and hunted separately under their own chiefs. Before the Plains Indians had horses, they traveled on foot. They moved slowly, about six miles a day, the speed of a dog dragging a loaded travois.

A band marched in military formation. Scouts went ahead of the main body to search for buffalo and a campsite.

The buffalo hunt. Artist J. M. Stanley has captured the moment when a brave is preparing to put his spear into the side of an angry buffalo. Notice that he's riding bareback, without saddle or stirrups, and guides his horse only by the pressure of his knees against its sides.

Behind them walked the tribal chiefs carrying medicine bundles to frighten away evil spirits. Next came the women carrying their bundles and hurrying the dogs along. The warriors, whose responsibility was to prevent surprise attacks, marched behind the band and along its sides.

When buffalo were located, the band made camp nearby, but not near enough to frighten the grazing animals. Experienced hunters studied the herd, making their plans according to its movements and the lay of the land.

The object of the hunt was to kill the most buffalo within the shortest time. One way to do this was the "surround." The band's travois were wedged upright in the ground and tied together to form a corral with a narrow entrance. A group of hunters then set fire to the grass around the herd, surrounding it with a wall of flame except for a pathway to the corral. The trapped animals crowded together and were slaughtered with spears and arrows. As many as three hundred buffalo could be killed within ten minutes by this method.

The "buffalo jump" brought even better results. A band camped along a riverbank overlooked by high bluffs. On the morning of the hunt, everyone climbed to the top of the bluffs to get into position. On the plain they saw piles of rocks and earth that had been put there years before. These strange mounds were arranged in two lines that began at the edge of the bluff and branched out in a long V-shape. The mounds at the bluff's edge were about two hundred feet apart, those at the far end about a half-mile apart.

The people hid behind the mounds, peering out now and then to see what was going on. What they saw might have made them laugh, had it not been so serious. A buffalo herd grazed in the distance. Between it and the wide opening of the V was a skilled hunter, the Buffalo-Caller. He was on his hands and knees, covered with a buffalo robe; a stuffed buffalo head covered his head. His every motion was a perfect imitation of a buffalo bull. He snorted. He pawed the ground. He rolled in the dust.

Time dragged for the anxious onlookers. No one spoke, but just held his or her breath and prayed.

Meanwhile the herd was getting curious about the strange "buffalo" nearby. A cow left the herd to have a closer look. Another followed, then another, until the whole herd was

A buffalo jump was a large, open-ended V-shape at the top of a cliff. Indians then drove hundreds of the frightened animals over the cliff to their death on the rocks below.

moving slowly toward the Buffalo-Caller. And he moved further into the V.

Suddenly the Indians stood up and began to shout and wave blankets. The animals panicked, those in the rear pushing those ahead of them forward. By the time the Buffalo-Caller ducked behind a mound, the first animals had tumbled over the edge. Within minutes the whole herd went over the cliff, bellowing and kicking in the air. That night the camp's drying racks creaked under the weight of a fresh load of buffalo jerky.

The coming of the horse was as important to the Plains Indians as learning to hunt buffalo. Unlike the buffalo, the horse is an Old World animal first brought to the Americas by the Spanish explorers. As the Spaniards advanced northward from Mexico in the 1600s, they built ranches in what are today the states of Arizona, New Mexico, and Texas. They were not always careful with their horses, and many broke loose and headed for the open grasslands. These runaways were the ancestors of the wild mustangs that once roamed the plains.

Gradually the wild horses themselves changed. They grew smaller, because they now ate grass rather than grain. An all-grass diet, however, is very nutritious and the mustangs developed great speed and strength. They could run faster, turn quicker, and take care of themselves better than the heavier grain-fed animals of the settlers.

Within ninety years (1680-1770), all the tribes from Texas to Canada had become "horse Indians." It was love at first sight. To them, the horse was no ordinary animal but a "Spirit Dog," a "Medicine Dog," a "Holy Dog." Surely, they thought, this marvelous creature was a gift from Wakan Taka.

The horse allowed the Indian to travel faster and farther than ever before. He could venture anywhere on the grass sea

24

without being afraid. And his wife could set down her bundles. She rode, while a horse pulled everything, including the smaller children—in a brushwood cage tied to the travois poles. Although a dog could pull a seventy-five-pound load six miles a day, any horse could pull three hundred pounds twenty miles.

Horses were a man's most valuable possessions. The more horses he owned, the more respect he enjoyed in the tribe. Owning many horses meant that he was a sharp trader and skilled at capturing the fastest mustangs.

It also meant that he was a successful thief. Horse stealing was both a sport and an occupation with the Plains Indians. It took plenty of courage, skill, and luck to sneak into an enemy camp at night and get away with a prized animal. Such a person was admired in the same way that we admire sports stars. A wise man always kept his best horse close to him. When enemies were near, he slept with its rope tied to his wrist, so that the least motion would awaken him. He might even take the horse into the tipi, forcing his wife to sleep outside in the cold. To kill a man's best horse was the same as murdering a member of his family.

No Mongol, Cossack, Arab, or European knight could outmatch the Plains Indian on horseback. He learned to sit on a horse before he could walk. As soon as an infant outgrew the cradle-board, his father put him in front of him whenever he went riding. Or he was tied to the back of a gentle horse, which an older child led in circles for a few hours each day.

When he turned five, his father gave him a horse of his own. If he was thrown, well, that was too bad. He didn't dare cry, and nobody gave him sympathy. He just got up, brushed off the dust, and remounted. At eight or nine, his father sent him to care for the family's horses.

Work? No, this wasn't work for a healthy boy. It was heaven. He spent whole days alone with as many as five hundred horses. A favorite way to pass the time was to gallop after a horse with his lasso. It would dodge and buck, its hoofs flinging clods of dirt into the youngster's face. Catching it at last, he mounted it bareback and went after another horse, and another, until the sun set.

Friends liked to race their horses and play "Throw-Them-Off-Their-Horses." The boys chose sides, stripped naked so as not to give the other fellow anything to grab, and charged. The object of the game was to wrestle an opponent off his horse. Anyone who fell to the ground was "out." He might really be out—knocked out. Bruises and sprains were common. Yet boys heal quickly, but the lessons learned about riding stayed for life.

Horse and rider were a team. A well-trained horse trusted its master and would do anything he commanded. It dashed into the center of a buffalo herd, dodging and weaving to stay clear of the slashing horns. Since the Indian needed both hands to fire a gun or use a bow and arrow, he had to let go of the reins. No matter. The horse knew where its master wanted to go by the pressure of his knees and the shifting of his body weight.

An Indian boy of fifteen could do tricks that would make a champion rodeo rider green with envy. He leaped from the back of one horse to another while both were at full gallop. He reached down and picked small objects off the ground at twenty miles an hour; two riders could pick up a fallen brave without losing speed for an instant. He used his charging horse as a shield by dropping down to one side, holding on with only a heel hooked over its back and an elbow hooked into a buffalo-hair sling woven into its mane. This left his hands free to shoot a stream of arrows over the animal's back or from under its neck.

No wonder there were United States Army officers who would have given a year's pay to command such horsemen.

Plains Indian riders could hang over one side of their mounts so as not to expose themselves as a target to the enemy. Often, though, the cavalry simply shot down the horses.

"Give me the handling and discipline of such recruits as the Indian boys," said a veteran cavalryman, "and I can whip an equal number of any cavalry in the world." Maybe so.

The Plains Indian *was* a fearsome warrior. He hunted to live, but he lived to fight. War was his favorite pastime, his greatest joy and pleasure.

Describing war as a "joy" and "pleasure" seems strange until we realize that Indians and whites made war differently and for different reasons. The idea that people should always live in peace would have sounded strange, even silly, to the Indian. To him, peace and not war was unnatural. The Great Plains tribes were always at war. They passed on their wars from generation to generation as others handed down their family possessions. Sioux and Crow, Crow and Blackfeet, Comanche and Southern Cheyenne, Apache and Comanche, had been fighting for longer than the oldest people could remember. They fought to defend their hunting grounds or to capture new ones; to revenge past attacks; to punish insults; to take more horses.

Yet their main reason for fighting had nothing to do with gaining material things or even with killing the enemy. Of course people were killed, and sometimes whole villages were wiped out. But killing wasn't the main objective.

The Plains Indians valued courage above everything else. Brave deeds made the warrior proud of himself and brought him the highest honors of his tribe. Nor was he shy about his accomplishments. Far from it. Whenever given the chance, which was often, he boasted about his victories.

Nobody minded his boasting, even after hearing the same story for the hundredth time. A brave man was supposed to boast, for that way people were reminded that he was a special person—a "brave." A successful warrior was asked for his advice. He served on the tribal council, where all important decisions were made, and his neighbors chose him to lead in the tribal ceremonies. And he could marry. No woman would become the wife of one who hadn't proven his manliness in battle.

The Plains tribes had a "ladder of honor" which valued each war deed according to the danger involved. Killing an enemy might not bring any honor, since a coward can shoot a hero from ambush. Scouting ahead of a war party, however, took courage. So did stealing a horse from an enemy camp at night, leading a war party, and rescuing the wounded.

The bravest thing a warrior could do was to "count coup" on an enemy. Coup (pronounced "coo") is from the French word for "blow" or "hit." Counting coup meant going up to an enemy and deliberately touching him. A brave could slap his face or tap him with a long, thin wand called a coupstick. He could pull his weapon out of his hands or grab feathers from his war bonnet. Doing these things took courage, because a living, alert enemy was dangerous.

Coup could also be counted on the dead. Shooting an enemy brought no credit unless the brave rushed up and touched the body. If someone beat him to the touch, that person claimed the honor. Most tribes allowed three warriors to count coup on a single body.

Touching the fallen enemy brought honor because it was dangerous. Indians always tried to recover their dead, and some of the hardest fighting took place around the bodies of dead braves. Often the "dead" were very much alive, pretending in order to draw the enemy close enough to count coup on him.

The first warrior to touch a fallen enemy gave a victory cry at the top of his voice. "A-he! A-he!"—"I claim it!" What he claimed was the honor of taking the enemy's scalp. Many Indian ways seemed cruel in the eyes of white people. Yet the Indian believed them necessary for his own good.

They had noticed that hair is the only part of the human body that grows to any large extent over a person's lifetime. It grew, they believed, because it was a continuation of the person's spirit. Scalping was a way of capturing an enemy's spirit and preventing his ghost from taking revenge.

A brave took a scalp by grabbing the hair with one hand and cutting a circle around it with a knife. A quick jerk brought it away from the skull. The scalp was then dried and preserved on a pole kept in the warrior's tipi. Clumps of human hair were also used as fringes to decorate shirts and leggings. The only enemies who weren't scalped were those who committed suicide and Negro soldiers of the United States Army. Negro hair was usually short and tightly curled, "bad medicine" to the Indian.

A brave wore feathers for the same reason that a modern soldier is awarded medals. A feather, like a medal, told everyone at a glance that the wearer had done something worth remembering. A warrior who had counted coup described his deed to the tribal council. He brought witnesses to back up his claim. If the council agreed, it awarded him one golden eagle tail feather. The golden eagle was no ordinary bird, but the Sun Bird, the highflying messenger to the spirit world.

Eagle feathers were prized possessions. Braves dyed them various colors and notched, cut, and split them in various ways. Each design had its own meaning. A red feather, for example, was the Indians' Purple Heart, an award for being wounded in action. When a brave accumulated enough feathers, he made them into a war bonnet. Some famous warriors had double-tailed war bonnets that could only be worn on horseback to keep them from dragging on the ground.

Every boy was expected to become a warrior. Preparation for war was part of the normal hunter's training. Boys played war games, counted coup on each other, and held up clumps of buffalo hair in place of scalps. They learned that a warrior must be courageous and bear pain without flinching or crying out. He must be willing to sacrifice himself to warn the tribe of the enemy's approach. The members of the Sioux Kit Fox warrior society sang:

> *I am a Fox.*
> *I am supposed to die.*
> *If there is anything difficult,*
> *If there is anything dangerous,*
> *That is mine to do.*

To be a warrior meant to be a man. Anyone who found that he didn't have what it takes to follow the warpath stopped being a man and became a "woman." He put on women's clothing and moved in with a brave to help his wife with her chores. Such a man-woman was called a *berdache* and was never allowed to marry.

Each brave made his own weapons as he had been taught to do by his father. Knife, tomahawk, lance, and stone-headed war club were simple and deadly at close range. The bow and arrow was a long-range weapon. A finely made bow was of wood backed with thin layers of buffalo horn glued on and wrapped in sinew for added strength; the bowstring was also of sinew. Arrows were tipped with bone or flint. White traders exchanged steel arrow heads for buffalo skins.

The bow and arrow could be as deadly as any gun. It was a silent weapon, allowing the warrior to strike without giving away his position. It could also be fired faster than the single-shot muzzle-loaders used before the Civil War. A skilled bowman could keep eight arrows in the air at once. And they usually hit their mark. He could bring down an enemy at two hundred yards. At fifteen yards, he could send an arrow clean through a buffalo or hit a door knob.

The Indian never mastered the white's gun. Although he bought guns and took them from the dead, there were never enough to go around. During the biggest battles, fewer than one brave in four had a rifle or pistol. Those who did couldn't repair them when broken or count on having enough ammunition. Bullets were hard to get and each kind fit only one type of weapon. They were too valuable to be used in target practice. As a result the whites were, man for man, better marksmen, especially at longer distances.

Real Indians, unlike movie Indians, seldom charged into battle by the thousands. Big battles in the open were too costly, and the tribes too small, to afford to lose so many lives at once. They preferred to fight in small groups called war parties. The smaller the war party, the better its chance of catching the enemy off guard and escaping safely.

31

Anyone could organize a war party if he could persuade others to follow him. A warrior was a free person, and nobody could get him to fight against his will. He went with a war party because he trusted its leader, a warrior with many coups or a war chief. Each tribe had several famous warriors whom everyone respected. Although a chief, he was no general, for he couldn't give orders to anyone. The war party decided for itself when and how to attack. If a warrior's spirit-helpers visited him in a dream and told him to go home, he went home without anyone thinking him a coward. During battle the war chief shouted advice and led by his own example. Each brave decided for himself whether to follow or ignore the advice.

War parties always set out at night after a war dance in which everyone wished them good luck. Comanche warriors sang songs to their wives and sweethearts that any American soldier fighting in the World Wars would have understood:

> *Going away tonight;*
> *Be gone a long time.*
> *While I'm gone,*
> *I'll be thinking of you.*

A week or two later, deep in enemy territory, he prepared for battle. His guiding rule was: Take no unnecessary risks. The Indian fighter understood that courage was not the same as going out of your way to get hurt. That's stupidity.

His favorite tactic was the surprise attack, usually at dawn, when people are less watchful. If the plan worked, many coups were counted and scalps taken. If it failed, the attackers rode away as fast as their horses could carry them. There were no fights against long odds, no last-ditch fights to the finish. Braves felt no shame in running away and living to fight another day.

As the eastern sky turned purple with dawn's first light, the braves dressed for battle. They dressed by taking clothes off, not by putting them on. Clothes meant more weight for their horses to carry, thus slowing them down.

Paint took the place of clothing. The Plains Indians loved bright colors, and the brighter the better. Every woman painted a red line in the part of her hair. Red was a sacred color tying her to the earth, which bears fruit in season, as she hopes to bear healthy children. Men painted their faces at all times. Paint was the Indian's suntan lotion and insect repellent. It protected him against sun, wind, and horseflies, whose bite feels like an electric shock.

A warrior would sooner have left his weapons behind than go into battle without painting his face and body. Dazzling patterns of lines, dots, circles, zigzags, and lightning bolts were not intended to frighten the enemy. These designs were exciting and beautiful, not ugly; they were magical armor given to him in dreams by his spirit-helpers for protection and to increase his warrior powers.

Each color had its own meaning. Scouts, for example, painted their faces white, for the wolf, who knew every trail in enemy country. Red meant bravery, which is why the early explorers called the Indians "red men" and "redskins."

The Indian's war horse was also decorated. Eagle feathers were tied to its tail and red circles painted around its eyes to give it speed and sharp vision. Other designs told of its master's past victories. A rectangle meant that he had led a war party. Straight lines, one above the other, were coup marks. The outline of a hand stood for an enemy killed in hand-to-hand combat in the same way that a fighter pilot paints a tiny flag on his plane for each enemy shot down. A painted horse was really a galloping billboard advertising its master's brave deeds.

The last thing a warrior did before riding to battle was

White-Man-Runs-Him, a Crow scout who worked for the Army, wore paint to give magical protection and to tell others about his accomplishments as a warrior.

to uncover his shield. A shield gave two kinds of protection. Its layers of thick buffalo hide could stop any arrow. Bullets had to hit it straight on or they'd fly off at an angle. But above all, the shield was a sacred object full of magical power. Its design, like those on the warrior's body, had been given him in a dream by his spirit-helpers. This design was supposed to give better protection than any thicknesses of buffalo hide. The warrior kept his shield covered until the last moment, because showing it too soon would cause its magical power to blow away like smoke.

If the raid succeeded, the war party galloped into its home camp whooping and waving scalps. That night the women held the scalp dance, or "Hair-Kill Dance." Hour after hour they danced around a fire, singing and waving the trophies tied to long sticks.

A war chief had a lot of explaining to do if he lost even one man. How was the brave killed? Could his death have been avoided? Many questions were asked and they had to be answered; there could be no cover-ups. If he was careless or gave bad advice, the dead man's family cursed him, even killed his horses and tore down his tipi.

The fallen warrior's face was painted in his favorite pattern and his body dressed in the finest clothes. The body was not buried in the ground, but wrapped tightly in buffalo skin and placed on a specially built scaffold or in the fork of a tree. Next to him were placed weapons and food for the journey to the next world. There, in the Milky Way, his spirit became a tiny star glowing warmly in the cold darkness of the night. Long-lost relatives welcomed him, and together they hunted buffalo forever.

Plains Indians lived exciting, satisfying, self-respecting lives. But that wagon train of July, 1859, was a sign that things were turning topsy-turvy.

The *Wasichus*—white people—were already swarming across the Plains. At first most of them followed the Oregon and Santa Fe Trails to the Pacific coast and the lands of the Southwest. Even though they were just passing through, their wagon trains upset the Indians' way of life. These *Wasichus* seemed to have no respect for nature. Their garbage began to foul the crystal-clear streams. Their gunfire drove the buffalo away from the ancient hunting grounds. Settlers killed buffalo, took the best parts, and left the rest to rot in the sun.

Yet this was only the beginning. Wagon trains soon began to stop on the plains. The *Wasichus* intended to stay! They built homes, and fences, and plowed under the grass. Miners slashed open the hillsides in search of gold. Towns sprang up where once the Indian had raced the wind.

The Great Plains were becoming too small for both the Indian and the settler. One had to go so that the other could use the land as he pleased.

And so began the thirty-years' struggle for the West. It was a struggle that the Indian never had the smallest chance of winning.

two

The Lords of the Southern Plains

Some of the most terrible battles in the wars for the West took place in the southern part of the Great Plains. Lying between the Platte and Rio Grande Rivers, this area today includes all or part of six states.* In the old days, before the *Wasichus,* four tribes controlled the area. The Southern Cheyenne, Arapaho, Kiowa, and Comanche were proud warrior peoples who meant to keep what they had.

Their troubles began in Colorado after prospectors discovered gold in 1858 in the Rocky Mountains near Pikes Peak. Indians called gold "the yellow metal that makes the *Wasichus* crazy." It certainly seemed that way, because whites poured into the territory as fast as they could; one hundred thousand came in 1859 alone. They came by pack mule, or on foot, carrying their own packs, or pushing wheelbarrows. Wagon trains decked out with banners reading "Pikes Peak or Bust" came from lands beyond the sunrise. Many did "go

* Nebraska, Colorado, Kansas, New Mexico, Oklahoma, Texas.

bust," while others struck it rich. Within two years one of their mining camps, a jumble of cold, leaky shacks, became the prosperous town of Denver.

The Indians' anger grew along with the settlers' numbers. Before long, war parties were setting out each night from Cheyenne and Arapaho encampments to attack the new-comers. Next morning the buzzards led searchers to the scalped body of a rancher or a miner who had foolishly gone out alone.

Not all whites were killed, or killed at once. Children, if

*Plains Indians attacking
the Butterfield Overland Stage.
These stages were often so
crowded that passengers
had to ride on the top. Everyone
was armed, for an attack was
to be expected.*

young enough, were often adopted by their captors and
raised as Indians. Women might be forced to do the heavy
work of a warrior's wife. Warriors sometimes married female
prisoners themselves. Their children, part Indian and part
white, were called "half-breeds," as were the children of white
fathers and Indian mothers.

Captured white men were never spared. It was the custom of the Plains Indians to torture prisoners to death. Braves
expected such treatment at enemy hands; they had spent most
of their lives thinking about it and preparing for it. It was

important not to give in to pain. For the more pain a prisoner took without crying out, the more he proved that he was better than his enemies.

The whites' greatest fear was being captured alive. Plainsmen had a saying, repeated again and again in wartime: "When fighting Indians, keep the last bullet for yourself." A quick bullet seemed better than being "staked out." The prisoner was laid on his back and his arms and legs tied to pins driven into the ground. Indians then roasted his legs and arms; finally, a small fire was built on his chest and kept burning until he could feel no more pain.

Settlers could understand why the Indians would fight to keep their lands. They couldn't understand, or forgive, kidnapping and torture. These actions deepened their hatred of the Indians and the belief that they were savages. "The only good Indian is a dead Indian," many said, so that little mercy was shown or expected by either side in the struggle for the West.

Small-scale fighting continued in Colorado until the summer of 1864. The Civil War had forced the United States Government to transfer most army units from frontier duty to eastern battlefields. There Union and Confederate forces tore at each other for nearly five years to decide whether the country would remain a united nation.

It was a bad time, that summer of '64. With the troops gone, the Cheyenne and Arapaho went on a rampage. Stagecoaches were ambushed, making it necessary for Denver to have its mail sent by boat around South America and over the Rockies from California. Supply wagons dared not cross the plains without armed guards, and there were never enough of these. Farmers abandoned their crops and streamed into Denver, which had become an armed camp. Things became so bad that John Evans, Governor of Colorado Territory, telegraphed Washington: "Our lines of communication are cut, our crops are all in exposed localities, and cannot be gathered by our scattered population. Large bodies of Indians are undoubtedly near Denver, and we are in danger of destruction both from the attack of Indians and starvation."

Evans's appeal for troops was turned down, as none could be spared from the Union Army. What he did get was permission to form a regiment of "Hundred Dazers," volunteers who joined for a hundred days at a time. These volunteers were not trained soldiers, but undisciplined civilians out to punish the Indians—any Indians, guilty or innocent.

Not all Indians were following the warpath. Black Kettle, chief of one of the largest Cheyenne bands, had done his share of scalping. But the years of fighting had convinced him that the whites couldn't be defeated and that the Indians'' best hope was to make peace as soon as possible.

A meeting was arranged between Black Kettle and Governor Evans. The governor wanted peace also, but only on his terms. Black Kettle's Cheyennes, he insisted, must surrender their weapons and move to a reservation. Until then, they'd be considered "hostiles," enemies, and attacked.

As Evans spoke, the Indians couldn't help moving their eyes back and forth from his face to a man standing nearby. He wore the blue uniform of an officer in the Union Army. The Indians had seen many Bluecoats, but he seemed different. There was something strange about him, something wild. A giant of a man, he stood over six feet tall and weighed at least two hundred and fifty pounds. Yet he wasn't fat. He was solid, a man-mountain of muscle with a thick neck and a barrel-chest. His face was a mass of black, wiry hair, like the beard of a bull buffalo. Gray eyes glared from above the curls.

Governor Evans finished his speech and, turning to the Bluecoat, asked if he had anything to add. The officer was Colonel John M. Chivington, commander of the Colorado Volunteers. A good soldier, Chivington had recently defeated

Colonel John M. Chivington commanded the Colorado volunteers during the Sand Creek Massacre of Cheyennes. His rule was "nits make lice," and even women and children must be killed.

the Confederates in New Mexico, saving that territory for the Union. Now he intended to save Colorado for the *Wasichus*. Chivington cleared his throat, staring hard at the Indians. His words were like icicles: "My rule of fighting white men or Indians is to fight them until they lay down their arms and submit to military authority." With that, the meeting ended. The Indians were satisfied, for they believed they had been promised protection as long as they stayed peaceful. They were wrong.

Neither the governor nor the colonel believed an Indian's promise. Those "redskins," they thought, understood only force, and that's what they'd give them. Black Kettle's band was camped along Sand Creek, a branch of the Arkansas River in southern Colorado. That camp would be destroyed as a warning to all Indians.

Chivington set out on the night of November 28, 1864, with seven hundred mounted men and four light cannon. His orders were simple: "Kill and scalp all, big and little; nits (insect eggs) make lice." Indians, to the colonel, were not people but evil creatures to be stamped out.

Chivington's command rode under a starlit sky. A cold wind nipped at the men's noses and cheeks. To keep warm, and also to keep up their courage, they drank whiskey. The raw "rotgut" alcohol made them angrier with each passing mile.

The volunteers were guided by a half-breed hired to locate Black Kettle's camp. He was worried and, near daybreak, he stopped. Turning to Chivington, he said, "Wolf he howl. Injun dog he hear wolf, he howl too. Injun he hear dog and listen; hear something, and run off."

The colonel scowled and tapped his pistol butt. "Jack," he said, "I haven't had an Indian to eat for a long time. If you fool with me, and don't lead us to that camp, I'll have you for breakfast." They found the camp.

Dawn was breaking when they came to the top of a low bluff. Below, a sleeping camp of about one hundred tipis was gathered on the dry streambed at a bend of Sand Creek. A horse herd grazed nearby. All was quiet, undefended, as in peacetime.

A Cheyenne woman, an early-riser, saw the troopers coming. Mistaking them for buffalo, she rushed through the camp shouting that a buffalo herd was stampeding.

The first shots told the Indians their true danger. Rushing from their tipis, they saw a group of white men drive off their horses with pistol shots, cutting off their escape. Black Kettle raced from his tipi, calling to his people to stay calm. The chief had a large American flag, a gift from a friendly soldier, which he hoisted over his tipi along with a white cloth as a surrender sign. Men, women, and children crowded around the flag, certain it would give them protection.

Chivington's men, ignoring the flag, blazed away with rifles and pistols. Cannon roared. Braves singlehandedly charged groups of raiders, hoping to slow them down to give others time to escape. Only a few made it to safety by running along the streambed.

It was a massacre. The raiders rushed forward, taking no prisoners. Wounded warriors were shot where they lay. Women and children, even babies, were shot and scalped. Four hours later, after the shooting stopped, three hundred Indians, mostly women, the young and the elderly, were dead, compared to fourteen whites. Black Kettle escaped, although his wife had been seriously wounded.

News of Sand Creek shocked the nation. Even amid the brutality of a Civil War, many Americans felt disgraced at Chivington's actions. Kit Carson, the famous frontier scout and Indian fighter, was angry. Said Kit. "To think of that dog Chivington and his hounds up thar at Sand Creek! Who ever heard of sich doings among Christians! The pore Injuns had our flag flyin' over 'em, that same old Stars and Stripes we all love and honor. Well, then, here comes along that durned

Colonel Chivington's cavalry attack Black Kettle's people at Sand Creek, Colorado. An artist has captured the scene at the moment the massacre began.

Chivington and his cusses. So they just pitched into these friendlies and massa-*creed* them in cold blood, in spite of our flag thar! And ye call *these* civilized men and the Injuns savages? Pore things!"*

But good words can't unto bad deeds. As Black Kettle's people fled to their Northern Cheyenne relatives, other Southern Cheyennes and Arapahos took their revenge. Roving bands

* Colonel Chivington escaped punishment for Sand Creek. When the Civil War ended, he resigned from the Army to go into politics in his native Ohio, whose voters never elected him to high public office.

destroyed ranches and wagon trains. A large force burned the town of Julesburg. Warriors derailed a train, shot the crew, and galloped across the plain trailing streamers of stolen red cloth.

The few Army units still in Colorado tried to control the Indians, but they easily escaped in the vast open spaces of the Great Plains. In desperation the soldiers set grass fires to destroy grazing for the Indians' horses and drive off game.

No one had ever seen anything like it before. The fires were started along the Platte River and whipped southward by the wind. A wall of flame thirty miles wide lunged forward, unstoppable. Showers of sparks allowed it to leap rivers. Animals in the millions fled before the inferno. Other millions of prairie dogs, nesting birds, and buffalo couldn't escape. The fire tore through Colorado, finally burning itself out in the Texas Panhandle. In spite of the damage to wildlife, the Indians, who were used to natural grass fires, simply got out of the way without loss.

Fighting continued for nearly a year. The Indians took their revenge, but fear of another Sand Creek remained at the back of their minds. And so, when the government sent a peace commission in October, 1865, they were prepared to listen to its terms. In return for peace, the Southern Cheyenne and Arapaho agreed to leave their lands and move to reservations where the government would feed them until they learned to be farmers. Unfortunately, the peace was only to be temporary. Nobody could say when war would return, or how, but everyone knew that it would return and that it would be a different kind of struggle. For next time the tribes would face their most determined foe: the United States Army.

The end of the Civil War (April, 1865) released American forces for frontier duty. The army that returned to the West

46

was nothing like Chivington's undisciplined volunteers. It was "all RA"—all Regular Army—professionals who had been through the greatest war ever fought in the New World. None of its assignments during the next quarter century would be more important than keeping the Indians in line.

The Indian-fighting army was special in many ways. From top to bottom, it was made up of men who had chosen the service as their life's career. Th end of the Civil War meant the end of the million-man army that had beaten the Confederacy. The government lost no time in discharging most of the troops and taking apart the expensive war machine it had built so carefully.

Cutbacks forced nearly all of the best officers to accept lower ranks or leave the service. Brigadier generals became colonels, colonels became majors or captains, and so on down the line. This meant that, for a generation, every officer above lieutenant was an experienced combat leader of proven ability.

Most ordinary Civil War soldiers left service cheerfully, glad to return to their families in one piece. Yet thousands of others found peace dull and routine after years of excitement. In spite of the dangers and hardships, the army drew them back, for danger also meant adventure, and where there was hardship there was also comradeship.

The army was America in miniature, drawing men from all nations and walks of life. An Austrian nobleman ate dust as an infantryman alongside a peasant's son. Germans, Frenchmen, Englishmen, Norwegians, Dutchmen, Russians, and others served in the ranks. But it was the Irish who flocked to the army. Big, husky men, they were courageous, no-nonsense soldiers.

The army also drew its share of ex-rebels who changed their Confederate gray for Yankee blue uniforms. Having done so, "Johnny Reb" might find himself serving in the same area as his former slaves. Blacks made fine, disciplined

soldiers who formed such crack regiments as the Twenty-fourth Infantry and the Tenth Cavalry. The Indians called them "Buffalo Soldiers," because of their curly hair and the buffalo design on their battle flag.

Indians, too, served in the Indian-fighting army. Some tribes disliked each other more than the whites. Joining the army as scouts allowed them to settle old scores and be paid for the pleasure by Uncle Sam. Pawnee, Crow, Shoshone, and Arikara gladly helped the army against their more powerful enemies among the plains tribes. They always fought bravely, alongside white and black troops.

The Indian-fighting army was based in ninety-seven forts that stretched from Canada to Mexico. In spite of movies and

*Fort Phil Kearny, Dakota Territory.
Unlike most frontier forts, which were of open
construction, this fort was surrounded
by a wooden palisade.*

television, only the smallest forts in the heart of Indian country were surrounded by a stockade of logs set in the ground
and sharpened at the top. All other forts were of open construction. Large numbers of troops, rather than stockades or
protective ditches, were their main protection. No army fort
on the Great Plains was ever overrun by Indians.

The typical fort consisted of rows of buildings arranged
around a parade ground to form a rectangle. Unmarried soldiers lived in long barracks on one side. Across the way were
married soldiers' quarters and the officers' cottages. Kitchens,
headquarters, hospital, guardhouse, and warehouses com-
pleted the rectangle.

Life at an army post took a lot of getting used to by

soldiers and their families. Climate was always a problem. You either froze in the northern or broiled in the southern plains. Texas, everyone agreed, was the worst assignment of all. General Philip Sheridan once said, "If I owned Texas and hell, I'd rent out Texas and live in hell." The soldiers agreed. They used to tell of a comrade who died and went to hell, only to return a moment later for his blankets. Texas was much hotter!

Frontier living really tested a wife's devotion to her husband. The army wasn't in business to make life easy for married couples. Living quarters were small, drab, and impossible to keep clean. Coyotes howled all night, while rattlesnakes liked to snuggle up to a sleeping person on a chilly night. During winter blizzards, buffaloes would take shelter behind the fort's buildings. The sound of the wind howling mixed with the moaning, scraping, and rubbing of the buffaloes against the thin walls.

An animal's sniffing wakened a cavalryman's wife. Thinking it a dog, she offered it a piece of bread. A dark shape snatched it from her hand and burst through the half-opened door. A guard fired. She stared from the window, wide-eyed, at the body of a big wolf. Other uninvited guests included tarantula spiders, thumb-sized roaches, swarms of grasshoppers, and legions of stinging ants.

Army women had to be able to defend themselves, for a post might be attacked when most of the troops were away. At such times a woman with a gun was as valuable as any man. Husbands taught their wives to handle rifles and pistols. Tiny, frail-looking women became deadly shots with the .44-caliber pistol, even though it took both hands to keep it steady. Horseback riding was as much an amusement as a necessity, and all the army wives learned to ride. Women wore special riding dresses, never blue jeans or men's shirts.

Soldier's children were called "army brats," because they

were so high-spirited. Boys and girls, they had their own horses and were taught to ride and shoot. Friends might include sergeants with stories to tell, Indian boys, and, for the lucky few, Buffalo Bill himself.

The sergeants were the backbone of the army. The unmarried men were a rough bunch who needed rough discipline. A sergeant who couldn't "control by whistle, fist and boot" soon lost his stripes. The punishments he served out ranged from stiff fines to double guard duty in the broiling sun or freezing cold. Repeated rulebreakers wore the wooden overcoat, a barrel with its bottom knocked out and a hole cut in the top for slipping over the head. This device was heavy, hot, scratchy, and silly-looking.

The Indian-fighting army respected its opponents. Officers and men knew that the brave was as good a fighter as any of themselves. Still, as a fighting *team*, the army knew it was better.

Not that you'd know it by looking at the troops. They looked more like a mob of cripples and hoboes than professional soldiers. Many had old battle injuries that would never get them past a recruiter for today's army. There was a one-armed general followed by his one-legged assistant. Men with missing fingers and toes, shot off or frozen off in long-ago campaigns, were common in the ranks, as were men with one eye.

The cavalryman wore a slouch hat, oversize blue coat, baggy blue pants with a yellow stripe down each seam, high boots, and a bandanna knotted around his neck. Infantry and artillery dressed the same, except that their pants had a pale blue or red stripe on each side.

Although its troopers were well-armed and tough, the army's real strengths were its organization and discipline. These qualities could multiply a group's fighting power many times over. Yet the army's strengths were exactly its enemy's

Frederic Remington's painting shows a group of mounted warriors circling around a wagon train protected by soldiers fanned out in front. Two Indian horsemen, riding at full gallop, pick a wounded comrade off the ground.

weaknesses. The Indians had excellent warriors but no soldiers, plenty of chiefs but no generals.

The Indian brave was an individualist, a star who fought for his own glory in his own way. Stars had no place in the army. The soldier was a team player, trained to follow orders and fight as part of a group. Of course personal bravery was important, but discipline was all-important. The courageous man who couldn't work with the team soon lost his scalp.

Discipline and teamwork turned many a defeat into a victory. The Indians, for example, were experts at surprise attacks, but terrible at defending themselves against surprise

attacks. Lacking real commanders and group discipline, they usually broke and ran after the first shots. Not the soldiers, whose tight discipline helped them recover from a surprise, reorganize, and counterattack.

Their idea of leadership was also different. The Indians had lots of war chiefs but not one big chief everyone had to obey—or else. Chiefs never had an overall war-winning plan, nor did they look beyond the next raid or battle. Victory had to come swiftly and cheaply, otherwise they retreated as fast as possible.

The army, though, had a high command able to see war

as a big picture and plan its moves in advance. A commander's interests went beyond winning any one battle, for his real aim was to destroy the enemy's war-making ability altogether. This meant setting a goal and sticking with it in spite of the cost.

Generals expected their troops to take heavy losses at certain times. Yet they kept after their objective. And so did their soldiers, whose discipline, pride, and loyalty to each other wouldn't let them quit.

The army needed all its stubbornness in dealing with the southern plains tribes. By 1868, the Cheyenne and Arapaho were on the warpath once again. Those who had fled north after Sand Creek began to return to their old lands to hunt and attack whites. Reservation Indians, who still longed for the free-roving life, were also restless. The Great Spirit had made them hunters and fighters, not diggers in the dirt. War parties, sometimes whole bands, escaped the reservations to join their friends.

They gave the cavalry a run for its money. As long as the braves kept to hit-and-run raids, they were safe. The "horse-soldiers" ran themselves ragged trying to track them down. War parties set out with two or three horses per man. After a raid, they kept moving nonstop, changing to fresh mounts whenever necessary. A war party could cover vast distances, leaving the cavalry to plod along until it lost the trail.

The army's leaders were furious at their troops' poor showing. William T. Sherman, the army's commanding general, and Philip Sheridan, commander of the frontier forces, had learned their trade during the Civil War. Both men believed that harshness was the best policy in war. Not only must the enemy's soldiers be defeated, his civilians must be made to suffer as much as possible, they believed. Said

Army strategy was to attack the Indians in the middle of the winter, when they couldn't use their advantage of mobility to escape over the Great Plains. Here Custer has rounded up tribesmen and is driving them to captivity across the frozen plains.

Sheridan: "The people must be left with nothing but their eyes to weep with."

Both commanders resolved to stop the Indian raids quickly, brutally, and permanently. Their plan was simple; indeed, Colonel Chivington had stumbled upon it at Sand Creek without realizing that he held the key to victory. The Indians had to be fought when they couldn't escape—in the wintertime. With the plains buried in snow and lashed with sub-zero winds, the tribes lost their great advantage, their mobility. Their horses, forced to paw the ground to get at the frost-covered grass, grew thin and weak. War parties could not move about as quickly or cover the same distances as before. Everyone, warriors and their families, was imprisoned in camp during blizzards.

Bad weather for the Indian was good weather for the army. The cavalry were all-weather soldiers. Railroad trains slammed through the snow drifts, bringing tons of food, ammunition, and warm clothing. And since their horses ate farm-grown oats rather than wild grasses, they could go anywhere in winter.

Large bodies of cavalry were to leave camp at night, during blizzards if necessary. They would scour the countryside for hostile bands, attacking them without warning. Their orders were not only to shoot the braves, but to destroy the bands' ability to fight in the future. Tipis, buffalo robes, blankets, clothing, stores of pemmican, and hunting gear were to be burned. The Indians' horses would be shot. The people would be turned out to wander the frozen plains, homeless, hungry, and cold. When they grew tired of having nothing but their eyes to cry with, they'd beg to be allowed to settle on a reservation.

General Sheridan chose for the job the Seventh Cavalry led by his friend, a young Civil War hero named George Armstrong Custer. Colonel Custer's target was a large band of southern Cheyenne known to be wintering along the Washita River in western Oklahoma near the Texas border.

Before dawn on November 23, 1868, a bugle sounded at Camp Supply, Oklahoma, a dingy, lonely supply base of tents and shacks.

"Prepare to mount," it signaled.

"Mount."

Instantly seven hundred troopers swung into the saddle. Custer, a flaming red bandanna around his throat, nodded, and the band struck up *The Girl I Left Behind Me*, a snappy Civil War marching tune. Then, with the thermometer reading ten below zero, the Seventh Cavalry rode into the teeth of a raging blizzard.

The column rode through the blizzard for three days and nights, stopping only to rest and eat cold meals of canned pork and hardtack, a dry bread so hard it sometimes had to be broken with pistol butts. Each man rode alone, unspeaking, enclosed in his own frosty envelope; Custer had ordered the column to move as quietly as possible. Icicles dangled from mustaches. Now and then a trooper squirmed to make the lice moving between his body and clothing change position. Only the creaking of leather saddle gear and the dull thud of hoofs on the snow marked the column's progress across the barren landscape.

A few minutes after midnight, November 27, Custer and his officers followed Scout Little Beaver to the crest of a low ridge. Peering over, they saw a large black blotch moving across the moonlit snow: a horse herd. "Heap Injuns down there," Little Beaver whispered. A moment later a dog barked, followed by a baby's shrill cry. That cry echoed in Custer's heart, pleasing him and troubling him at the same time. He was pleased that he had found the enemy and could already taste victory. Yet he was also saddened. For the Custers were childless and never would have children. That innocent baby seemed to be crying for him—and his soldier's duty was to destroy its village.

Custer divided his force into four groups, each to strike the village from a different side when he gave the signal. The only thing left to do now was to wait patiently and silently for sunrise. Smoking was forbidden, for the aroma of tobacco smoke carried far in the clear air. No man could speak above a whisper or stamp his feet to keep warm.

Black Kettle's village slept peacefully below. Even after Sand Creek, Black Kettle continued to call for peace. He could call, but, like any Indian chief, he couldn't command.

Warriors from his band had been attacking whites all summer. In fact, white prisoners were in his camp that night, along with fresh scalps and messages take from army couriers who had been ambushed.

The village slept soundly except for a lone guard, Double Wolf. More guards weren't necessary, the warriors believed, since no one could fight in such weather. Double Wolf sat in front of his tipi, watching the moonlight reflecting off the snow-covered ridgeline. A baby wailed for a moment. A dog barked. Double Wolf went into his tipi to warm his hands over the dying fire and, moments later, was asleep.

Time dragged for the waiting cavalrymen. Small groups stood about, whispering about the coming fight. Others lay on blankets in the snow with their horses' reins wrapped around their wrists. A good soldier will try to sleep anywhere and on anything.

The sky was brightening as the sergeants moved among the men with final orders. Each soldier had to take off his overcoat and leave it in camp, because the bulky garments would only be in the way during the fight. Quietly they mounted and began to advance over the crest of the ridge and down through the light timber on the other side.

A Cheyenne woman had risen early to gather firewood along the river. Suddenly she saw something move above her. Cavalry! Her cries startled Black Kettle awake. Running from his tipi, he saw the troopers approaching, but this time he knew there was nothing to talk about. He raised his rifle and fired a single shot.

Custer was turning in his saddle to give the attack signal when he heard a shot echoing off the hillsides. "Play!" he shouted to the regiment's bandleader. Trumpets blared a few bars of "Garry Owen," the Seventh Cavalry's marching song, then fell silent as the players' saliva froze in the mouthpieces. Still, those few bars were enough.

Shouts and cheers rose from the camp. All units were in position and charged at once, pistols barking. The cavalry's favorite weapon was the Colt .44-caliber pistol. This six-shooter was fourteen inches long, weighed three pounds, and packed a terrific wallop at close range. Although heavy, it was lighter and easier to handle than a rifle or sword, which was almost useless in Indian fighting and usually left behind

The first shots downed Black Kettle and his wife as they tried to escape. The troopers sped past their bodies and stormed into the camp, firing as they went. Heavy horses ran into tipis, knocking them down in a tangle of wooden poles and buffalo skins.

The startled Cheyenne ran from their camp nearly naked and without moccasins on their feet. (Tipis were warm inside, and Indians slept without clothes so as not to be bothered by the bugs that infested their buffalo robes.) People plunged into the icy river, wading downstream in water up to their shoulders. Braves carried small children over their heads to keep them from drowning.

Although individuals fought desperately, sacrificing themselves to cover the others' escape, Black Kettle's people offered no organized resistance. One boy, no older than fourteen, earned the admiration of Captain Frederick Benteen. Seeing Benteen advancing at the head of his squadron, the youngster drew a pistol and charged. Benteen, not believing his eyes, raised his hand in a peace sign. Two shots whizzed by the captain's head. Still he kept his hand up in peace. That was a brave boy whose life deserved to be spared. A third shot struck the captain's horse, forcing the officer to fire in self-defense. The troopers' admiration, however, quickly turned to anger after they found the bodies of a white woman and two children who had been killed to prevent their rescue.

Custer, meanwhile, was beginning to feel uncomfortable. He noticed that the Indians' gunfire was increasing rather than

dying down. Worse, he saw
hundreds of braves in war
paint and war bonnets gathering in the hills nearby. At
last he learned from a prisoner that Black Kettle's people weren't alone. Nearby,
also camped along the Wa-
shita, were thousands of
Southern Cheyenne and Arapaho, plus bands of Kiowa
and Comanche. They had
taken in the survivors of
Black Kettle's camp and were
now out for revenge.

Custer was in a tight spot,
but he had been in tight spots
before. He knew that if he
retreated openly, the braves
would crush the rear of his
column. He decided to borrow an Indian hunting trick:
when faced by a dangerous
animal, it is sometimes better to look it in the eye and advance
boldly. That's what the Seventh Cavalry did. Toward evening,
Custer had the band strike up a snappy marching tune and
move straight toward the Indian villages downstream. As the
braves fell back to defend their homes, he gave the order to
about-face and march back quick-time. Only at dawn did the
Indians realize that the enemy had slipped away.

The battle of the Washita wasn't another Sand Creek
massacre. There was no deliberate shooting of women and
children or scalping, except in one case. Yet Cheyenne losses
were high: one hundred and three killed, compared to twenty-

George Armstrong Custer leads his men in the attack on Black Kettle's band camped along the banks of the Washita River.

one cavalrymen. When Custer withdrew he also left behind a charred mass of hundreds of tipis, blankets, moccasins, pots, pans, bows and arrows; tons of pemmican and jerky; and the bodies of eight hundred and fifty-seven horses shot by his men.

The battle of the Washita broke enemy resistance, convincing them that the Army would do anything to have its way. Within two months, the remaining Southern Cheyenne and Arapaho bands reported to Fort Cobb, Oklahoma, for settlement on reservations along the Washita River. Never again would they challenge the cavalry.

The Kiowa and Comanche, meanwhile, had begun their last ride down the warpath. These tribes lived between the Arkansas and Red Rivers, a huge territory that included the Texas Panhandle. The Comanche especially were famous as horsemen and warriors. They owned more horses than any other tribe. One Comanche band of two thousand people had over fifteen thousand horses, while some chiefs owned a thousand horses, nearly all of them stolen. No wonder it was said that the Comanche were "half-horse and half-man."

The Comanche and their Kiowa allies were experts at raiding and horse stealing. During the "nights of the Comanche moon," when the bright September moon lit the way, war parties poured southward along a five-hundred-mile trail marked with horses' bones. The Comanche hated the Texans, having fought them long before their territory became a state. The Texas Rangers were originally formed to fight the Comanche on their own terms, at close range on horseback. War parties also raided Mexico, scalping, burning, and returning with horses and captured women and children to hold for ransom or adopt into the tribe.

In October, 1867, the United States Government sent a peace commission to win over the Kiowa and Comanche. At Medicine Lodge Creek, Kansas, they agreed to settle on a reservation near Fort Sill, Oklahoma, in return for yearly payments of money, food, and clothing.

The *Wasichus* soon discovered that persuading Indians to move to a reservation was easier than keeping them there. Both sides were at fault for what followed. The government sent less than promised, causing food shortages and making the Indians feel cheated. The braves, for their part, missed the excitement of the warpath. Since the reservation was so large, war parties easily slipped away to raid settlers, returning in time to collect their government-issued rations.

Who were the raiders? Where did they come from? Settlers said they were "reservation-jumpers" out on a lark. Government officials, safe in Washington, thought the settlers were exaggerating.

At last, in the spring of 1871, General Sherman decided to find the truth for himself. After leaving the steamboat at New Orleans, Louisiana, he went on to Texas by road in an army ambulance fixed up as a traveling coach and escorted by a squadron of cavalry. The burned ranch houses and freshly dug graves he passed convinced him that the settlers hadn't exaggerated.

Although Sherman didn't know it at the time, he almost filled one of those graves himself. As his caravan neared Fort Richardson in northern Texas, it passed in front of a low hill behind which two hundred Kiowa braves were waiting in ambush. At the head of the war party rode Satanta—White Bear —the most famous Kiowa chief. A six-footer, he seemed tall as a bear, and as strong, with muscles rippling along his arms and shoulders. Bright red war paint covered his face and body, glistening in the sunlight.

The Kiowas could easily have wiped out the small caravan, had they known who rode in the ambulance and had their medicine man not heard an owl, his spirit-helper. An owl had hooted, meaning, he said, that they must attack only the *second* group of whites to come along the road that day. Thus General Sherman kept his red hair, thanks to a restless owl. An hour later, though, some Army supply wagons were attacked and nearly all their drivers killed. When Sherman heard of the attack, he ordered cavalry from Fort Richardson to find the Indians and report to him at his next stop, Fort Sill.

General William T. Sherman was Commander in Chief of the United States Army after the Civil War and a mastermind of the strategy against the Plains Indians.

It so happened that Satanta and his band arrived back at the reservation at the same time as the general. No one would have been the wiser had Satanta been able to keep a secret. But keeping quiet about a successful raid wasn't his way. He boasted about the killings to anyone who'd listen, Indian or white. Next day he received an invitation to meet with Sherman at the Fort Sill headquarters building.

The Kiowa chief Satanta committed suicide after being sent to prison for massacring a group of Army wagon drivers in Texas.

Satanta and his accomplices, Chiefs Satank and Big Tree, sat cross-legged on the porch facing the Bluecoat officers, who sat on chairs. Only Sherman stood. Back and forth he paced the porch with hands clasped behind his back. He looked like a ferocious eagle. A lean man, he had a deeply lined face, a bristly beard, and cold, gray eyes.

Satanta, still bragging, amazed everyone by admitting to

the raid and telling how he had some of the wagon drivers tortured. Sherman, cool as ever, stopped pacing only long enough to announce that the Indians were under arrest and would be tried for murder.

"I'd rather be dead," said Satanta as he drew a pistol from under his blanket.

Sherman nodded. Instantly the shutters along the porch flew open, revealing groups of Tenth Cavalry Buffalo Soldiers in each window. Their faces were grim as they aimed their rifles at the Indians. A bugle call summoned more Buffalo Soldiers, mounted and armed, from the stables to cover the front of the building.

Sherman, meanwhile, continued to pace the porch, unaware that his life hung by a thread. A brave named Stumbling Bear had quietly fitted an arrow to his bow, intending to die while bringing down the soldiers' big chief. He was bending his bow when an officer glanced upward, saw him, and nudged his arm so that the arrow swished harmlessly past Sherman's ear. Buffalo Soldiers quickly disarmed the chiefs and hustled them off to the guardhouse.

Everyone breathed a sigh of relief, except Sherman. The veteran of a dozen near-misses only shrugged his shoulders and said, "We came near to having a row."

Next day, as the Kiowa chiefs were being driven to trial in Texas, Satank was shot while trying to escape. Satanta and Big Tree were convicted of murder and sentenced to life in prison. Although Big Tree was later pardoned, Satanta jumped from a high window rather than be caged for the rest of his life.

At the very moment Satanta and Sherman had their showdown, events were taking place far away to the east that would threaten the Plains Indians' whole way of life. Except for a

Satank, Satanta's accomplice in the massacre of Army wagon drivers, was shot while trying to escape on the drive to Texas, where he was to stand trial.

small market in buffalo-skin robes and overcoats, until 1871, white people had not been especially interested in the animal. In that year, however, a Pennsylvania tannery found a way to turn buffalo hide into fine leather for shoes, saddles, and furniture. Overnight buffalo hides were worth three dollars apiece, more than a factory worker earned in a week. The buffalo was doomed.

Hunters fanned out north and south from Dodge City, Kansas, a key railroad link to the east. Armed with high-powered rifles, they had no trouble shooting the lumbering beasts. The buffalo is as stupid as it is large. Hunters found that once its leaders were shot, a herd would wander in circles until all were dead.

Champion buffalo hunters held contests to see who could kill the most within a given time. William F. Cody earned the nickname "Buffalo Bill," because he shot over four thousand animals in just a few months. Cody once challenged a hunter named Billy Comstock to a contest to see who would be champion of champions. Eight hours later, Buffalo Bill proved that he was the best with a score of sixty-nine to forty-six.

Buffalo Bill and his fellow hunters slaughtered the buffalo by the millions. They were joined by "sportsmen" who took cut-rate excursion trains into the heart of buffalo country. As the trains chugged along slowly, the hunters fired repeating rifles from the windows. Soon the Plains became a vast open-air graveyard littered with skeletons, skulls, and rotting carcasses. The sour smell of death hovered over the plains, polluting the fresh air.*

* The buffalo herds of the Southern Plains were completely wiped out by 1878; the Northern Plains herds vanished by 1883. Only thirty-four buffalo were alive in the West by 1903.

Everyone knew that when the buffalo disappeared the Plains Indian would also have to disappear or give up his old way of living. He'd have to stop being an Indian and become a farmer, a grubber in the soil. The Comanche and their Kiowa cousins meant to save the buffalo so that the Indian might live.

Quanah Parker was the half-breed son of Cynthia Ann Parker, a captured white girl, and a Comanche chief. Quanah was brave and intelligent, and by the age of eighteen had become war chief of the Kwahadi Comanche, a band that had never signed a treaty with the whites or lived on a reservation. Quanah now sent word: To save the buffalo, the buffalo hunters had to be destroyed.

Comanche, Kiowa, Arapaho, and Cheyenne braves rallied to Quanah from everywhere. When he had seven hundred men, he headed for Adobe Walls, a hunters' trading post in the Texas Panhandle just west of the Oklahoma border.

Before dawn, June 27, 1874, the warriors swept toward the trading post in a mass charge. Charging this way was a mistake, for the noise of hoofbeats awakened the twenty-eight hunters. During the precious seconds that remained, they took up positions at the building's windows, doors, and on the roof.

Twenty-eight against seven hundred are long odds, but not impossible ones. The hunters fought from behind adobe walls, sunbaked clay thick enough to stop anything except a cannon shell. Best of all, their hunting rifles had telescopic sights that allowed them to knock a brave out of the saddle a half-mile away. Bullets flew thick and fast until Quanah's men withdrew with the bodies of fifteen of their comrades; left behind were another twelve whose bodies couldn't be removed, plus two whites killed at the beginning of the fight.

Indian anger boiled over after the defeat at Adobe Walls.

Quanah Parker of the Comanches had an Indian father and a white
mother. His people were among those rounded up in the Palo Duro
Canyon campaign by Ranald Mackenzie.

War parties attacked any whites they could find, forcing the government to rush thousands of fresh troops to Texas.

And then the attacks stopped, suddenly, without warning or, it seemed, without reason. An eerie quiet settled over the southern plains. Gone were the buffalo, whose stampedes had shaken the earth. Gone also were the Indians. By mid-July more than half the Comanche and Kiowa had run away from the Fort Sill reservation. Patrols were sent out to find them, but returned empty-handed. It was as if the earth had swallowed the Indians.

The earth had, in a way, done just that. The Indians had gone to join the last remnants of the buffalo herds at a secret place, Palo Duro Canyon. The Palo Duro is a huge gash in the earth in northwestern Texas, near the present city of Amarillo. Carved by a branch of the Red River, the canyon is more than eight hundred feet deep, although only about five miles wide at the bottom. Invisible from the horizon, the Palo Duro was a paradise of sparkling water, cooling shade trees, and abundant grass.

Thousands of Comanche, Kiowas, and other Indians gathered here in that summer of 1874. They came not as war bands, but as families to grasp their last chance to live in the old way. Hunters killed only enough buffalo to meet their needs. Women carefully prepared pemmican for the winter. Children swam in the streams, giggling and laughing as they played familiar games. Horses—over two thousand of them—munched the grass. No one, Indian or animal, would ever again know such joy in freedom.

In the meantime, telegraph receivers chattered in scores of army posts. General Sherman was sending his orders.

Find the runaway Indians.

Destroy their possessions.

Round up the people and send them back to Fort Sill.

He'd accept no explanations, no excuses, for failure.

He wanted results.

Period. End of message.

Five columns of cavalry set out from forts in Colorado, Kansas, Oklahoma, New Mexico, and Texas. They went back and forth, scouring the countryside, their trails crisscrossing again and again. On September 24, 1874, a column led by Colonel Ranald Mackenzie stood at the rim peering into the winding Palo Duro.

The Indians' worst enemy had been their feeling of safety. No guards had been posted to give the alarm in case enemies should appear.

Most of Mackenzie's cavalry had already made it down the narrow trail into the canyon when the Indians realized their danger. As usual, the braves covered the retreat of their women and children, then fled themselves.

No matter. Mackenzie had already achieved his main objective. Once again all the Indians' belongings went into the bonfires. Over fourteen hundred horses were rounded up and shot.

The Indians might escape the cavalry, but the winter, which came early in 1874, punished them worse. Men and women, young and old, suffered as never before. Exhausted, they wandered over the snowy wasteland searching for shelter and a mouthful of food. Barefoot, they left bloody tracks in the snow.

Gradually bands of half-naked, starving Indians turned themselves in at Fort Sill. Whatever meager belongings they still had were heaped up and burned. Their remaining horses, now pitiful bags of bones, were run out onto the prairie and shot. The next spring, after Quanah Parker brought in his Kwahadis, no Indian lived freely anymore on the southern plains.

Colonel Ranald Mackenzie was a Civil War hero who led his cavalry against the Comanches in the Palo Duro Canyon of Texas.

Less than a year later, in the spring of 1876, some dust-covered Colorado cowboys drove their longhorns down the narrow trail to the floor of the Palo Duro. Piles of sun-bleached horse bones lined the way, unnoticed by the thirsty cattle.

The Indians were gone, locked up in reservations.

The buffalo herds were gone, destroyed forever.

The future was clear that beautiful day. The new lords of the southern plains would be the rancher, the cowboy, and the longhorn.

WASHINGTON

GROS VENTRES, PIEGAN

FLATHEAD

Marias R.

BLOOD, CROW

Milk R.

CROW MONTANA

OREGON

Missouri R.

Yellowstone

CROW

BATTLE OF
LITTLE BIG HORN
Fort C. R. Smith ■

IDAHO

Rosebud R.

Tongue

Little
Big
Horn R.

Fort
Ph

SHOSHONE

Big Horn R.

WAGON BOX BATTLE

North Platt

WYOMING

NEVADA

Walker Lake

UTAH

ARIZONA

NEW MEXICO

CALIFORNIA

Rio Grande

FORTS AND BATTLES

❋ BATTLES
■ Forts

▦ INDIAN
RESERVATIONS

NORTH DAKOTA

SIOUX

ARIKARA
GROS VENTRES
MANDAN

Bismarck

Fort A. Lincoln

MINNESOTA

Fort
Ridgely

MINNESOTA

SIOUX

Acton

MASSACRES

Wood Lake

New Ulm

Mankato

SOUTH DAKOTA

SIOUX

Missouri R.

Black
Hills

Cheyenne R.

White R.

BATTLE OF
WOUNDED
KNEE

Ridge Agency

Fort Laramie

Wounded Knee Creek

NEBRASKA

IOWA

Platte R.

COLORADO

Republican

MISSOURI

KANSAS

Fort Leavenworth

R. R.

BATTLE OF
SAND
CREEK

Sand Creek

Kansas

Fort Lyon

Arkansas R.

OKLAHOMA

BATTLE
OF ADOBE WALLS

ARAPAHO, CHEYENNE

ARKANSAS

Canadian R.

BATTLE OF
THE WASHITA

Ft. Cobb

Palo
Douro
Canyon

ARAPAHO

Washita R.

TEXAS

three

A People Called Sioux

August 17, 1862, was an ordinary Sunday in southwestern Minnesota. The forested hillsides lay peaceful under the summer sun, while an occasional breeze carried the strong scent of pine into the drowsy valleys below.

Services were under way in the tiny church at Lower Sioux Agency near Fort Ridgely. The congregation, mostly farmers with calloused hands and dirt under their fingernails, fidgeted in their stiff Sunday-go-to-meeting clothes.

Also present were a few converted Indians, among them Little Crow, a leading chief of the Santee Sioux. Everyone there knew him, liked him, trusted him. And, for his part, the sixty-year-old chief thought of himself as a friend of the whites. He had visited Washington, D.C., several times at government expense to see the sights and discuss his people's problems with officials of the Bureau of Indian Affairs. No one knew it that morning, least of all Little Crow, but in a few hours he would take charge of the most dreadful Indian massacre in American history.

Chief Little Crow of the Santee Sioux led the greatest Indian
massacre in American history against the settlers of Minnesota.

Little Crow's people belonged to the Sioux or Dakota nation, the largest (about fifty thousand people) and most powerful of the Great Plains tribes. At the height of their power, the Sioux* controlled the Northern Plains from the headwaters of the Mississippi River to the banks of the Yellowstone and Powder Rivers.

The word Dakota means "allies," for the Sioux were divided into three branches. Seven branches made up the Teton Sioux, or "Dwellers on the Prairie": Oglala, Hunkpapa, Miniconjou, Brule, Sans Arc, Two Kettle, Sihasapas. The Teton Sioux roamed the open grasslands, hunting buffalo and raiding smaller tribes, like the Crow. To the east, centering along the Missouri River in present-day South Dakota, were the Yankton Sioux. The Santee, or woodland Sioux, were based in Minnesota, a country not only of grasslands but of rolling hills and forests dotted with lakes.

Minnesota was too rich and beautiful to be overlooked by the whites. Settlers poured in, along with fast-talking government agents eager to have the Santee sign away their lands. "Thim bald-headed ould divils" is how a veteran cavalry sergeant described these men from Washington. Yet they succeeded, and in 1851, the Santee gave up over thirty million acres in return for a reservation along the Minnesota River and a yearly payment of seventy thousand dollars.

The Indians never saw more than a tiny fraction of their money. Dishonest traders hovered around the Santee like hungry buzzards. Not that they stole outright; they were too clever for that. Instead, they stole quietly, with pencil and paper. Goods were sold to the Indians on credit, payable

* The people called Sioux never used this name for themselves. Their old enemies, the Chippewas, called them *Nadouessioux*— rattlesnake. The early French-Canadian traders shortened it to Sioux (Soo).

when the money arrived from Washington. Not only did they charge high prices and forge account books, they sold goods that were unfit for human use. Moldy flour and rotten bacon were all right for Indians, they said, although they wouldn't dream of feeding such slops to their own families. When the Indians complained to their agents, government officials appointed to protect their welfare, they ruled in favor of the tradesmen, who often slipped them a few dollars in appreciation.

The Santee controlled their anger until 1862, the worst year so far. Insects ruined the corn crop. Game was scarce, due to overhunting by whites. Hunger became widespread and the Indians faced starvation unless help came soon.

Help didn't come. The government was busy with the Civil War and officials had forgotten to send the money due that year. Reservation warehouses, meanwhile, bulged with unsold supplies. The Santee asked if the tradesmen would let them have more credit, taking payment whenever the money arrived.

No, they wouldn't extend any more credit. In fact a storekeeper named Andrew Myrick declared, "If they're hungry, let them eat grass for all I care."

Eat grass! The Santee repeated Myrick's words to one another, spitting them out like bitter roots. A proud people with long memories, they vowed to avenge this insult some day.

That day, a warm Sunday in August, came sooner than anyone expected. At about the time Little Crow was heading home from church, four Santee braves strolled into a farmyard fifty miles to the north. They found two families, the Joneses and Bakers, enjoying a day in each other's company. The braves' sudden appearance hadn't surprised or frightened them; armed Indians were a common sight in frontier Minnesota.

*Survivors of the Minnesota massacre rest for a while under armed
guard after fleeing from the rampaging Sioux.*

After exchanging greetings, the Santee challenged the
farmers to a target-shooting match, a challenge gladly accepted since they were growing tired of small talk. The farmers shot first, then stood aside without reloading their rifles.
That mistake cost them their lives. For instead of aiming at
the targets, the braves turned and fired, killing three men and
two women. By evening the four were boasting of their
"heroic" deed in their village.

What should Little Crow do? The young men clamored for a general uprising. They had had enough of hunger and insults, they said. Besides, only cowards would turn their people over to the whites for trial. No Santee had ever had a fair trial in a white court.

Little Crow spoke out for peace. "Braves," he pleaded, "you are like little children; you know not what you are doing. See! The white men are like the locusts when they fly so thick that the whole sky is a snowstorm. Kill one, two, ten, and ten times ten will come to kill you. Count your fingers all day long and white men with guns in their hands will come faster than you can count. Braves, you are little children. You are fools. You will die like rabbits when the hungry wolves hunt them in the Hard Moon of January." Then, lowering his voice in sadness, for they meant to have war no matter what he said, the chief murmured, "Ta-yoa-te-duta (Little Crow) is not a coward; he will die with you." They were his people and he couldn't let them down even though he knew they were wrong.

Little Crow's warriors took the whites completely by surprise. At dawn on Monday, as settlers began to stir from their beds, braves swooped down on Lower Sioux Agency. Mr. Andrew Myrick, storekeeper, was the first victim. As he lay dying on the ground, braves pulled up clumps of grass and stuffed them into his mouth, chanting "Myrick is eating grass himself."

The uprising spread like a forest fire, sweeping an area fifty by two hundred miles. Wherever one turned that morning pillars of smoke could be seen rising from farmhouses and haystacks. Whole families, including young children, were wiped out at their breakfast tables or in ambushes along the roads. Among the victims were recent German immigrants who spoke no English and knew nothing of the Indians' wrongs.

Over two hundred settlers were killed on Monday alone, the number climbing to six hundred forty-four by week's end. Hundreds more, women and children, were captured. Fear, pain, and hunger were all they'd know for weeks to come.

The lucky ones who escaped would remember their experiences always. Mrs. Lavinia Eastlick lost her husband and three eldest sons during a raid. Although wounded herself, she managed to hide with her eleven-year-old son, Merton, and Johnny, her baby, in the tall weeds along a stream. Santee

Eleven-year-old Merton Eastlick carried his baby brother, Johnny, to safety after his mother was wounded and told him to flee. They were reunited accidentally, and safely, several days later.

braves were all around, yelling and searching for them. As they drew near, Mrs. Eastlick told Merton to save his brother no matter what happened. Merton, his heart pounding, his head reeling, snatched up Johnny and ran just as the braves found their hiding place.

Merton lost track of time during the next few days. Barefooted, the skin of his feet worn to the bone, he hid by day and ran by night, sharing only wild berries with his baby brother. Just as his strength was giving out, he fell into the arms of—his mother! Mrs. Eastlick had slipped away from the Indians at the last moment and met a mailman who was taking her to safety in a town fifty miles from their original hiding place.

The Santee might have hurt the settlers even more had they followed Little Crow's advice. An attack on Fort Ridgely was high on the list. This fort was not only a refuge for fleeing settlers, but the gateway to the valley of the Mississippi River all the way to St. Paul. If that gate was forced open, nothing could stop the Santee west of the Mississippi. But Little Crow's braves had other ideas. Rather than attack the fort on Tuesday, they insisted on rampaging over the countryside, attacking easy targets like isolated farms that still hadn't heard of the uprising.

Delay gave the whites time to prepare their defenses. By Tuesday evening Private William Sturgis was digging his spurs into his horse's sides as they sped toward Fort Snelling one hundred twenty-five miles to the east. Like Paul Revere, he sped through the darkness, stopping in river towns only long enough to shout the alarm and call the citizens to arms.

Sturgis had left in the nick of time, for at sun-up a lone figure rode toward Fort Ridgely from the west on a beautiful high-stepping horse. It was Little Crow and he rode back and forth waving a blanket, the signal for a meeting.

It was a trick. While all eyes were turned toward him,

eight hundred Santee warriors dashed out of the woods to the north. On they came, impatient to get at the fort's one hundred fifty defenders and the three hundred settlers crowded in there for protection.

Fort Ridgely was of open construction with buildings lined up on each side of a parade ground. The north side had a stone barracks building in front of which stood a row of log houses, the fort's first line of defense. Little Crow's men easily broke through this line and captured the barracks beyond. The place became a madhouse of gunshots and screams as they hurled the defenders across the parade ground. The helpless civilians, expecting to be massacred any moment, were gripped with panic.

When all seemed lost, one man saved the day. His name was Sergeant John Jones and he wore the red pants-stripe of the artillery. Fort Ridgely had been an artillery post until its modern cannon were transferred to Civil War battlefields in the east. Only a few rusty cannon nobody thought good for anything were left behind.

Nobody except Sergeant Jones. He loved those old guns and couldn't stand by while they rusted away. During his spare time he scrubbed and polished them until they shone; he even taught some younger soldiers the fundamentals of gunnery as a way of passing the time.

Suddenly hundreds of lives depended upon these amateur artillerymen. As the Indians rushed across the parade ground, Sergeant Jones had three cannon wheeled into position. Sweating crews rammed gunpowder charges down the barrels, followed by bags of grape shot, canvas bags filled with five hundred musket balls apiece.

The Indians, sensing victory, kept coming. Closer. Closer. Closer they came to the waiting cannon.

"Fire!" Jones shouted.

BOOM. BOOM. BOOM. Loud thunderclaps rose above

the battle's noise, followed by the *whoosh* of fifteen hundred musket balls slicing through the air. The cannon had become gigantic shotguns.

One of the Indians' worst weaknesses as fighters was their inability to stand up to the fire of "wagon guns," as they called cannon. Brave as they were, the noise seemed too loud, the flame and smoke too terrifying, to be man-made. Surely, they thought, there were demons in those long, shiny tubes. Little Crow's braves halted in their tracks.

The cannon spoke again. This time the braves fled in panic, leaving a hundred of their friends dead in the buildings and on the parade ground. The gate to St. Paul and the Mississippi slammed shut, closed by a sergeant who loved some old cannon.

Yet the Santee were far from admitting defeat. On Saturday morning, August 23, five hundred warriors rode out of the woods near the town of New Ulm. They moved at a slow trot, spreading out like a huge fan as they came onto the prairie. Streaming war bonnets, bodies streaked with paint, and brightly colored shields could be seen from the distance. The trot increased to a gallop, then, became a breakneck charge.

The defenders of New Ulm, all two hundred fifty of them, were ready. The battle raged throughout the day, first on the town's outskirts, then in the streets and among the buildings. Checked for the moment, the Indians set many buildings on fire to create a smoke screen. Again and again they raced through the smoke and sparks—into a hail of rifle bullets. Sundown came and they drew off, leaving New Ulm a heap of charred rubble.

Exhausted but alive, the townspeople dug trenches and tried to get some sleep, expecting to have to fight for their lives again next morning. Dawn came, and they thanked God they were wrong. The Indians were gone.

Reinforcements marched into Fort Ridgely a few days

later, to be greeted with hugs, kisses, and tears even from hard-bitten veterans. Leading the column was Colonel Henry H. Sibley, an experienced frontiersman and Minnesota's first governor. Sibley took his time, building his fighting strength day by day. At last, on September 19, he set out with sixteen hundred Regular Army troops and volunteers in search of Little Crow.

The Santee chief had been losing influence ever since the defeat at New Ulm. Many lesser chiefs quarreled with him openly, questioning his leadership. Sibley's advance made them realize that time was running out. Some wanted to flee to their Teton cousins on the Great Plains. Some wanted a last all-or-nothing battle. Some favored returning their prisoners in exchange for peace. "Stop fighting," one chief cried. "No one who fights with white people ever becomes rich, or remains two days in one place, but is always fleeing and starving."

The "all-or-nothings" won the vote and lost the battle. On September 23, Sibley's troopers, backed by "wagon guns," shattered the Santee at Wood Lake fifty miles upstream from Fort Ridgely.

Little Crow's power was gone. He hadn't wanted war at the beginning, nor did he want defeat once the fighting began. Now he had both: war and defeat. He was as angry with himself and his people as with the whites. There was nothing left to do, he said, but massacre the prisoners and escape across the Plains. Again he lost. Four hundred prisoners were given up in the hope that Colonel Sibley would show leniency toward the defeated Indians.

Sibley had no kindness in his heart for Indians, only hatred and a desire for revenge. Hundreds were rounded up and tried by military courts for war crimes. It took about five minutes for the juries to bring in guilty verdicts in each of three hundred seven cases, all of whom were sentenced to be hung.

President Abraham Lincoln, however, wondered about five-minute jury trials. He ordered the court records sent to the White House for him to examine one at a time. The sentences of all except thirty-eight braves whose crimes were clearly proven were set aside by Presidential order. These men were hanged on December 28, 1862, in the largest mass execution in American history.

The Sioux were finished in Minnesota. Early next May, a steamboat carried the first group of Santees on the first part of their journey to a reservation in Oklahoma. From now on they'd know barren brown soil and prickly pear cactus instead of lakes and lush green hillsides.

Little Crow never shared his people's new life. There was no pardon for him. In July, two hunters found the fugitive eating wild berries and shot him without warning.

The Santee defeat was the beginning, not the end, of the Sioux wars. Hundreds of Santee slipped through Sibley's dragnet and took refuge with their western cousins. These Sioux bands, especially the Oglala, had their own grievances against the whites. The Oglala were guardians of the best hunting grounds remaining on the Great Plains. The Powder

Thirty-eight Santee Sioux Indians were executed from the same scaffold at Mankato, Minnesota, December 26, 1862, for their part in Little Crow's uprising.

River country, as it was known, took its name from the area's main river. Lying between the Black Hills and the Big Horn Mountains of South Dakota and Wyoming, this land was a hunter's heaven. The last large buffalo herds grazed here. Elk, deer, and antelope roamed freely, abundant as nowhere else in the United States. Trout-filled streams of cold melted snow tumbled from the Big Horns, a spur of the Rockies, watering valleys covered with silver aspen, willow, and cottonwood. Wakan Taka smiled upon the land, and his people smiled, too.

A Sioux encampment along a river on the Great Plains about 1890. The tipis were always placed in a circle to allow for easy communication and defense.

The Soux might have continued to enjoy this land had not gold, the whites' crazy-making metal, been discovered in 1862 in the mountains of Montana. Fifty million dollars in pure gold were pulled from the earth within four years. Helena, Virginia City, Bannock and Bozeman, Montana, rose from nothing to become thriving settlements.

These towns had to be supplied with everything, since they produced nothing except gold dust and headaches for lawmen; gunfighters, bandits, and claim-jumpers flocked to the area. Wagon trains lumbered over the Oregon Trail, a dangerous, roundabout route through the Rockies. What the miners needed was a direct route from Fort Laramie, Wyoming, to shorten the journey by five hundred miles.

That route was opened in 1862-1863 by John Bozeman and John M. Jacobs. The Bozeman Trail ran northward from Fort Laramie, passed beneath the eastern slopes of the Big Horns, then turned westward to the Montana gold towns. Settlers soon called it the "Bloody Bozeman." Rather than see their country invaded and their hunting grounds ruined, the Sioux fought back by ambushing wagon trains and killing prospectors.

The government decided to protect the Bozeman Trail with a chain of army posts. In June, 1866, agents from Washington called a council at Fort Laramie. Americans, they said, didn't want to fight Indians or harm their hunting grounds; they wanted only peace, and were prepared to pay for it with money and gifts. All the Sioux had to do was allow the army to go ahead with its plan for the forts.

As one of the government agents was speaking, a long line of wagons arrived at the fort. The wagon train belonged to the army and, from its appearance, its mission seemed far from peaceful. Colonel Henry B. Carrington, its commander, said openly that his orders were to build forts along the Bozeman Trail.

The Indians were shocked. They had come to Fort Laramie in good faith, and now the army was announcing that it would build forts no matter what they wanted. The Sioux were whispering among themselves until Red Cloud rose to speak. A tall man of forty, with a thin face and an eagle's-beak nose, Red Cloud was the leading chief of the Oglala Sioux. His strength and luck were legends among his people. As a young man a Pawnee arrow had been shot through his body, from front to back, so that only the point and feathers were visible. These were broken off, and for the

Chief Red Cloud of the Oglala Sioux was the only Indian leader in the West to win a war against the United States Army. He is holding a pipe made of catlinite, a soft red stone, which the Indians believed was sacred.

next week he struggled for life without medical attention or drugs to relieve pain or prevent infection. He suffered silently, but soon recovered his full strength.

Red Cloud's words came fast and hot. "Look!" he shouted, pointing to the silver eagle insignia on Colonel Carrington's shoulder straps. "Here is the White Eagle who has come to steal a road through the Indian's land! The Great Father (the President) sends us presents, and wants us to sell him the road, but the white chief comes with soldiers to steal it, before the Indian says yes or no! I will talk with you no more. I and my people will go now, and we will fight you!" Drawing his blanket over his shoulders, the chief stormed out, refusing to accept the smallest gift from the government. Next morning the Indian camp was empty. It was war.

Colonel Carrington's caravan moved north, creaking and mooing, along the Bozeman Trail. It brought along everything from a thousand head of cattle to two hundred twenty-six wagons loaded with weapons, tools, plows, seeds, doors, window frames, locks, butter churns, and instruments for a twenty-five-man band. Officers' wives and children rode in the ambulances.

The column's first stop was Fort Reno, a tiny outpost of log buildings, where it got its first taste of what Red Cloud had in store for the invaders. Toward sunset, whooping, blanket-waving braves drove off dozens of horses and cattle. After leaving fresh supplies, Colonel Carrington moved on to build Fort Phil Kearny and a smaller post, Fort C.F. Smith, seventy miles up-trail. Both forts were named for Civil War heroes.

Fort Phil Kearny stood on high ground between the forks of Big Piney Creek, a branch of the Powder River. Colonel Carrington took Red Cloud's warning seriously and surrounded it with an eight-foot palisade of sharpened tree trunks. The nearby woods were cut down to give the defenders a long-distance view and a clear field of fire. The result was one of the strongest forts ever built on the frontier.

Fort Phil Kearny had to be strong, for Red Cloud had plenty of trouble in store for its defenders. Messengers galloped from his camp to spread the word: "The Powder River country is in danger. We must fight to save it!"

Help came. Black Bear brought his Arapaho. Northern Cheyenne, angry over Sand Creek, rode in by the hundreds. Hump arrived at the head of the Miniconjou Sioux. Gall of the Hunkpapa Sioux was there, along with Sitting Bull, who jonied them for a while during the warmer weather. Young Crazy Horse, the Oglalas' genius at planning ambushes, rode about on his yellow pinto pony, admired by everyone.

Red Cloud's men lost no time in putting their fighting skills to work. The fort's defenders seldom saw the enemy, but knew he was out there, always awake, always waiting for a chance to strike. One day grazing horses disappeared. Another day nearly all the cattle were run off, until fewer than a hundred remained. A sentry walking between two uprights on the palisade one night fell with an arrow in his back.

Collecting wood became a major military operation. Tons of wood had to be piled up not only for building but for cooking and to heat the fort during the winter. Woodcutting details went to the forest under heavy guard, but even then men were cut off and their tortured bodies found staked to the ground days later. A wise man at Fort Phil Kearny always kept close to his group and kept his head down. And he prayed that his commander wouldn't do anything silly, like challenging Red Cloud to an all-out battle.

Colonel Carrington, who had seen enough fighting during the Civil War to satisfy any ten adventure-seekers, did not believe in taking unnecessary risks. His job, as he saw it, was to build the Bozeman Trail forts and hold on with as few casualties as possible. Some of his younger officers, however,

were impatient with his caution. They were fire-eaters, scrap-
pers, who loved the excitement of battle. Even though outnumbered at least ten to one, they wanted to carry the fight
to the Indians. After all, they said, one United States Army
cavalryman was worth any ten Indians.

One such man was Captain William J. Fetterman, who
had more courage than brains. Fetterman started a whispering campaign against Colonel Carrington. The colonel, he
said, was soft, weak, afraid of Indians. A *man* could easily
whip the Sioux. And he, Fetterman, was surely a man. "Give
me eighty men and I'll march through the whole Sioux nation," he bragged. Captain Frederick H. Brown, due to be
transferred soon, agreed. Brown didn't want to leave the Wild
West without cutting a few notches into his rifle butt.

Their chance came on a cold, dreary morning, December
21, 1866. A woodcutting detail had set out for the forest when
a Sioux raiding party opened fire. The heavy wagons, which
had been moving in two parallel columns, were formed into
a circle to wait for reinforcements.

Sound carries long distances in the Big Horns and everyone at the fort knew about the attack instantly. The trumpet
blared "Boots and Saddles," sending men streaming out of
their barracks. A relief party formed on the parade ground
under Captain James Powell, who was a level-headed, take-no-
unnecessary-risks soldier.

As the gate swung open, Captain Fetterman rushed up
to the colonel. Since he outranked Powell, he demanded to
be put in charge of the relieving force. Carrington hesitated,
then gave in, but only after giving Fetterman a written order
to relieve the woodcutters and not chase the Indians beyond
Lodge Pole Ridge. "Yes, sir," said Fetterman, snapping a
smart salute. As the column passed through the gate, Captain
Brown rushed to catch up with it. Fetterman now had eighty-
one men under his command.

*Captain William Fetterman believed he was
smart enough and tough enough to defeat the
Plains Indians with a handful of men.
The result was the disastrous Fetterman Massacre
of December 21, 1866.*

The column was advancing quickly when a group of
mounted warriors cut across its path. The warriors waved
blankets to frighten the cavalry horses, daring the troopers to
come after them. Without hesitating, Fetterman disobeyed
his orders and set out after them across the forbidden ridge.

Ten warriors were in that little group: two Cheyenne,
two Arapahoes, six Sioux. Crazy Horse, their leader, had
planned a masterpiece of an ambush. He led his pursuers on,
always staying far enough ahead to be safe but near enough
to keep their interest. Whenever they slowed down, he slowed
down. Once he dismounted, pretending to pull a stone out

of his horse's hoof. Bullets flew overhead, but he paid no attention to them.

The decoys rounded the ridge, crossed a creek, and began to climb a hill still known as Ambush Hill. Fetterman's troopers followed. Suddenly Crazy Horse's men split into two groups, riding to the left and to the right, then turned to face the oncoming soldiers.

This was the signal the Indians had been waiting for. War cries shouted by thousands of braves came from everywhere at once. Braves in bright war paint and feather bonnets rose up from the gullies, from behind rocks, from over the crest of the hill. Foolish Fetterman had led his men into a trap.

Eighty men could not ride through the entire Sioux nation. Red Cloud's braves had few rifles, but guns weren't necessary at such close range. Lances and tomahawks flashed. The *twang* of bowstrings was followed by a dull *slap* as arrows struck flesh.

Soldiers ran for cover in a tumbled mass of boulders, but it was no use. Single-shot rifles couldn't be loaded fast enough to turn back the attackers. A gun cracked, an Indian fell, and three others took his place. Within minutes the battle became a desperate hand-to-hand struggle.

Some whites were braver than others. Captains Fetterman and Brown shot each other rather than face capture and torture. Not bugler Adolf Metzger, a gray-haired veteran of the Civil War. Metzger threw away his jammed rifle and used his bugle as a club until it was smashed out of shape. A burial detail later found his body fully dressed, unscalped, and covered with a buffalo robe. The Sioux knew how to honor bravery even in an enemy.

For the first time in American history a battle had ended without a single soldier surviving. The second no-survivor battle would be fought nine years later, about seventy miles away, along the Little Bighorn River.

Down in the valley the woodcutters, suddenly finding themselves alone, returned to the fort without losing a man. Colonel Carrington, meanwhile, had heard the distant gunfire and given the alarm. Guardhouse doors were flung open and prisoners returned to duty. Cooks, stablehands, and bandsmen dropped their work and grabbed their weapons.

Fetterman's disobedience had put the whole fort in danger, for there weren't enough men left to turn Red Cloud back if he made a full-scale atack. Night came, and everyone prepared for the worst. The women and children were placed in the fort's gunpowder magazine and a sergeant ordered to blow it up if the Indians seemed about to capture the fort. No one expected to live to see the next dawn.

Nature now took a hand in the battles of men. The temperature tumbled to thirty below zero and a blizzard roared over the Rockies. Snow fell in blinding white sheets, sending the Indians into their cozy tipis. The soldiers, however, couldn't rest or be warm, but spent the night shoveling away the snowdrifts that formed ramps to the top of the palisade.

Colonel Carrington knew that Red Cloud was waiting for the weather to clear before beginning his main attack. He had to send for help now, at the height of the blizzard, or the fort would be destroyed. And since telegraph lines hadn't yet been installed along the Bozeman Trail, someone had to deliver the message in person.

Any volunteers? John "Portugee" Phillips stepped forward: "I'll go, sir." Portugee Phillips was a fur trapper who worked for the army as a civilian scout. He had taken the hardest job of his life, a job where the odds were a million to one against him. For he had to ride two hundred thirty-six miles to Fort Laramie through Sioux patrols and a howling blizzard.

Phillips plunged through snowdrifts, sometimes riding,

sometimes leading his horse. He stood motionless for thirty minutes in the freezing darkness to make sure that a strange sound wasn't made by Indians. Cold stabbed through the woolen underwear, woolen shirt, pants, sweaters and buffalo overcoat he wore. Landmarks disappeared under a blanket of white, and he had no compass. Still his woodsman's instinct never failed. Southward, always southward, he moved through the storm, stopping only to feed his horse some oats and eat a few crackers and a handful of snow himself.

On the fourth night, he saw a light in the distance. Fort Laramie was celebrating Christmas with a big party. Officers in starched blue uniforms guided women in silk ball gowns around the dance floor at the officers' club. Candles lit up the party room bright as day. Logs blazed in the fireplace, spreading their warmth.

Outside, the Sergeant of the Guard challenged a lone horseman. Minutes passed, followed by a hurried knocking on the door.

Through the open door the dancers saw a dead horse lying in the snow and a figure that looked like a snowman rather than a person. Portugee Phillips was covered with snow from head to foot. His face was chalky-white, except for blue lips and red eyes. His beard and eyebrows were jagged with icicles.

Portugee Phillips handed over his message, and collapsed. The brave rider slept for three days, unaware of the excitement swirling around him.

Although fresh troops and supplies were rushed to Fort Phil Kearny, they weren't enough to break the grip of winter's cold or Red Cloud's warriors. Soldiers' morale tumbled when the War Department, blaming Colonel Carrington for Fetterman's defeat, replaced him with General Henry Wessels.

Life at the fort was hard, uncomfortable, and dangerous. One soldier recalled:

After the arrival of General Wessels, the winter continued one of unusual severity, with the thermometer down to twenty-five and forty degrees below zero most of the time. We had no fresh meat, no vegetables. We did get one small loaf of bread issued to us daily and enough for one meal, and after that was gone we had to fall back on musty hardtack, salt pork and black coffee. Occasionally we had bean soup. We had no place in barracks to wash, and after the creeks were frozen over we could not take a bath until they thawed out the following spring."

Winter gave way to spring, spring to summer, and still Red Cloud kept up the pressure. Not that he had an easy time, either. The army also had some tricks up its sleeve. In the supply wagons that rolled into the fort after Portugee Phillips's ride were wooden crates containing a type of gun new to plains warfare, the Springfield breech-loading rifle. The usual army rifle was a muzzle-loader; that is, a bullet was dropped down the barrel and put into firing position by tapping the butt on the ground or with a ramrod. Loading was time-consuming and dangerous, because the soldier had to stand or kneel to do the job properly, giving the enemy a good target. The slow rate of fire also allowed the enemy to rush in and kill with his bow and arrows while the soldier was reloading. In the breech-loader, however, a bullet was inserted into the "breech," an opening at the back, above the trigger, allowing the soldier to fire more quickly while lying on the ground or from behind cover.

The breech-loaders had their first test on the morning of August 2, 1867, when Captain James Powell led thirty-one woodcutters to a spot about six miles from the fort along Big Piney Creek. Powell, cautious as ever, had built an enclosure of fourteen wagon boxes, wagons with their wheels and bases removed. The enclosure was at once a corral for the detail's mules and horses, a storage area for supplies, and a small fort.

The woodcutters were at their work when, at 7 A.M., the lookouts' mouths dropped open in amazement. The surrounding hillsides seemed to move. Indians! No fewer than three thousand Indians were riding toward them.

Bullets were already kicking up puffs of dust as the soldiers dashed to the wagon boxes. Odd pieces of equipment —tools, barrels, sacks of grain, bags of beans—were hurriedly heaped up in the gaps between the wagons. Ammunition boxes were broken open and placed within easy reach, each soldier filling his hat with the heavy brass cartridges.

The troopers didn't have to wait long for the action to begin. Crouching in their wagon boxes, they saw a chief on top of a nearby hill—Red Cloud—raise his arm and bring it down sharply. The Indians came on in a thundering charge.

Sergeant McQuiery turned to Private John Grady, at eighteen the youngest trooper, saying: "You'll have to fight like hell today, kid, if you expect to get out of this alive." The odds were thirty-two to three thousand.

Captain Powell had time to shout only one order: "Men, here they come! Take your places and shoot to kill!"

Tongues of flames leaped from the wagon boxes as Red Cloud's braves came in range. Horses were hit, sending their riders diving headlong into the dust. The warriors kept coming, expecting the soldiers' fire to die down as they reloaded. Then they'd charge in and end the battle in five minutes.

But instead of slackening, the gunfire increased. Red Cloud, on top of the hill, couldn't hear individual shots coming from the soldiers' position, only a prolonged *RRR-I-P*, like the tearing of a huge bedsheet.

The Indians were bunched so closely together that two and sometimes three men were brought down by the same Springfield slug. Others took their places, sending a stream of lead into the troopers' position. Bullets hit the tops of the wagon boxes, followed by a loud crunching sound as splinters flew in every direction. Fire-arrows reached skyward, peaked, and came down trailing a banner of flame. These arrows set fire to piles of dry manure inside the corral, giving off a cloud of smoke. Burning manure combined with gunsmoke and dust to create an awful stench. Men's eyes watered. They sneezed uncontrollably. Some vomited over their shirt-fronts.

Although fighting for their lives, the soldiers could still admire the enemy's skill and courage. Sergeant Samuel J. Gibson later wrote:

> The whole plain was alive with Indians, all mounted and visible in every direction. They were riding madly about, and shooting at us with guns, bows and arrows, first on one side and then on the other of the corral. Then they would circle, and each time come in closer, uttering the most piercing and unearthly war cries. Some of the more venturesome would ride in close and throw spears at us. Others would brandish their war-clubs and tomahawks at us, and others, still more daring, would ride within a hundred yards, and then suddenly drop on the off side of their ponies, and all we could see would be an arm or a leg sticking above the pony's back, and 'whizz!' would come the arrows! They paid dearly for their daring, for we had a steady rest for our rifles, the Indians were all within easy point-blank range, and we simply mowed them down by by scores . . . . We witnessed the most magnificent display of horsemanship imaginable. Two mounted Indians would ride like the wind among the dead and wounded, and seeing an arm or leg thrust upward, would ride one on each side of the wounded savage, reach over and pick him up on the run, and carry him to a place of safety.

Six times the Indians charged, and six times they were hurled back with heavy losses. As they were massing for the seventh charge, a new sound came from the east, in the direction of Fort Phil Kearny. A cannon shell burst overhead, announcing a hundred-man rescue party. "We hugged each other in the ecstacy of our joy," wrote Sergeant Gibson. "We laughed, cried, and fairly sobbed like little children in the delerium of our delight." The battle was over, the Indians in retreat.

The Wagon Box Fight cost the army three killed and two wounded. No one can be sure of the Indians' losses. Captain Powell claimed in his report that over three hundred were killed and wounded. Red Cloud disagreed. Years later he told a newspaperman that over eleven hundred Indians had been killed and wounded. "It was a big fight," the old chief said with a sigh. "The long swords fought as I had never seen them fight before. My warriors were as numerous as blades of grass. I went in with many. I lost over half. The long swords fought true to the mark."

The Wagon Box Fight was over, but the raiding and sniping continued. Meanwhile, the government in Washington was losing interest in "Red Cloud's War," as it was now called. Once again peace commissioners were sent to meet with the Sioux at Fort Laramie. One April 29, 1868, the Indians agreed to stop fighting and move to a reservation in South Dakota. In return, the government recognized the Powder River country as "unceded" territory; that is, it would be Indian land forever. Finally, the Bozeman Trail was closed and the forts that had been built to protect it abandoned.

In July and August, 1868, long columns of troops and wagons streamed southward from Forts Phil Kearny, C.F. Smith, and Reno. Behind them they left empty buildings and crowded cemeteries. As the soldiers turned in their saddles for a last glance at the forts, they saw clouds of smoke billowing upward. Red Cloud's warriors were burning them to the ground.

Red Cloud's War was over. For the first time an Indian chief had won a war against the United States Army. But, Red Cloud's War was only a battle in the wider struggle. The army was gone—for now. The Powder River country was at peace—for a while. When the army returned, as it was sure to do, it would be to stay.

four

Sitting Bull and Custer

Red Cloud was a man of honor. Having won his war for the Powder River country, he lived up to everything he had promised in the Fort Laramie Treaty. He had promised to settle on a reservation, and he did. He had promised never to fight again, and he didn't, especially after he learned of the Wasichus' true power.

During a visit to Washington, the Sioux chief saw huge buildings of stone, not of buffalo skin like the Indian's tipi. At the Navy Yard he saw cannon with barrels wide enough for a small person to slip through. Like Little Crow before, he realized that his people could never defeat the whites permanently. "Our nation," he told a gathering of friendly whites, "is melting away like the snow on the sides of the hills when the sun is warm, while your people are like the blades of grass in the spring when the summer is coming."

Not all the Sioux saw things Red Cloud's way. When his band moved to the reservation, many Dakotas remained behind. Why should they live on a reservation? Had they fought

Chief Red Cloud in old age thinks back to the days that have passed forever. After years of fighting, he realized that, for him and his people, there was no road to follow except the white man's road.

so hard only to become reservation Indians living on others' charity? Let Red Cloud cower on the reservation. As for them, they had earned their freedom. The Powder River country was theirs forever, and they had a treaty to prove it.

The free Sioux followed the game as in the olden days.

They set up their tipis and hunted as if no world existed outside their domain. Yet they couldn't hold back the clock forever, and by the early 1870s they faced another invasion. As before, the strangers came seeking the crazy-making metal. Rumor had it that there was gold in the Black Hills. The rumors spread, bringing prospectors into the forbidden area.

The Black Hills were not only a hunting ground, but holy ground. The Sioux called them *Paha Sapa*, the center of the world, where young warriors went to speak to Wakan Taka and dream of the spirits. The fact that the land was sacred and that they had no legal right to be there didn't bother the gold-seekers. They came, and the Sioux scalped them, but others always followed in their footsteps.

The Great Father, President Grant, decided to do something before things got out of control. During the summer of 1874, Colonel Custer and the Seventh Cavalry were sent into the Black Hills to see if they really had gold and how much. An army invasion was the last thing the Sioux expected, and Custer's expedition did its work and withdrew before they knew what was happening.

Custer's report was a bombshell. Gold, deep, broad veins of the precious metal, laced nearly every hillside. Gold dust showed up even among the roots of the grass in certain places.

That's all the prospectors had to hear. This time they flocked to the Black Hills by the thousands, and nothing the government did could keep them out for long. Even a Washington official could see a massacre coming unless action was taken soon. The government's solution was simple: the Sioux must sell the Black Hills.

The Sioux's answer was short and sharp. *Paha Sapa* was not for sale. Not a blade of grass. Not a pinch of dust. Nothing was for sale at any price. And, to drive home their point, a group of Oglala warriors rode up to the government representatives firing their guns and singing in Sioux:

The Black Hills is my land and I love it,
And whoever interferes
Will hear this gun.

The government refused to take no for an answer. Treaty or no treaty, the Sioux had to give up the Black Hills. If they couldn't be talked out of them, or bought out of them, they'd have to be driven out of them. The Fort Laramie Treaty had become just another scrap of paper.

The government made its demands in a way sure to provoke another Sioux war. Late in December, 1875, messengers fanned out across the Powder River country with an official order: every Sioux must report to a reservation by January 31, 1876, or be treated as an enemy by the army.

The order was impossible to obey even had the Indians been willing to give up their land. The northern plains were in the grip of one of worst winters on record. No one in their right mind would venture across that frozen wasteland. Under-nourished horses were walking skeletons unable to pull heavy loads. Children and babies, the sick and the elderly, could never have survived a journey of hundreds of miles to the reservations.

Among the chiefs who refused to travel was *Tatanka Yotanka*—Sitting Bull. His name was known not only among his own people, the Hunkpapas, but throughout the northern plains. Every Indian knew of him and respected him. Born about 1831, he became a famous warrior, counting many coups while still a teenager. Yet he was more than a warrior. He was a natural-born leader with a gift for helping people work together.

Sitting Bull meant to fight, now that the *Wasichus* were breaking their promises. Early in the spring, when the grass again grew fresh and rich, he made camp in the valley of the Rosebud River in southern Montana; the Rosebud, like the

Sitting Bull, medicine man and war leader of the Hunkpapa Sioux in their war against the United States for the Black Hills.

Powder, Big Horn, and Little Bighorn feeds into the mighty
Yellowstone River. He sent messengers speeding to every
Sioux and Cheyenne band for hundreds of miles. The words
they spoke were his words: "It is war. Come to my camp at
the big bend of the Rosebud. Let's get together and have one
big fight with the soldiers!"

Young men, restless and angry, began to trade buffalo
skins for bullets and head for the Rosebud. Red Cloud told
his people to cover their ears, for Sitting Bull would lead
them to destruction. But even his own son, Jack Red Cloud,
rode away with the others.

A huge camp formed on the Rosebud, with hundreds of
newcomers arriving each week. Sitting Bull was elected high
chief of all the Sioux, for he alone seemed to have a winning
plan. He was everywhere, doing everything at once. He rode
among the people, singing war songs to strengthen their
courage. He gave advice, for he could only advise and not
command. "Go in small parties—two or three or four in a
bunch. Then the soldiers cannot catch you; they will not chase
you. Spare nobody. If you meet anyone, kill him and take his
horse. Let no one live. Save *nothing*!"

He also prayed to Wakan Taka for victory in the coming
battles. One day he climbed alone to the top of a high hill.
Gazing up at the sun, he cried out to the Grandfather Spirit:
"My God, save me and give me all my wild game animals.
Bring them near me, so that my people may have plenty
to eat this winter. Let good men on earth have more power,
so that all the nations may be strong and successful. Let them
be of good heart, so that all Sioux people may get along well
and be happy."

Returning to camp, Sitting Bull began the Sun Dance.
For a day and a night and most of another day he danced,
eating nothing, drinking nothing. At last he fell on the ground
and had a vision in which Wakan Taka showed him the

future. Soldiers, many soldiers, would come to harm the Indians, but they'd be destroyed. Three days later, June 17, 1876, the soldiers came.

General Sheridan intended to beat the Sioux with his favorite tactic of catching them between columns of troops closing in from different directions. Three columns would be used this time. Major General Alfred Terry would lead a powerful force westward from North Dakota to the Yellowstone. A second column under Colonel John Gibbon would move eastward along the Yellowstone from Montana. Finally, Brigadier General George Crook would follow the old Bozeman Trail northward from Wyoming until he reached the Yellowstone. The columns would meet near the point where the Big Horn River joined the Yellowstone, trapping the Indians and forcing them to surrender or be destroyed.

General Crook struck first on June 17. Crook, already famous for his campaign against the Apaches, got the surprise of his life from the Sioux. For on this day Sitting Bull had left the fighting to Crazy Horse of the Oglalas.

There was nothing crazy about Crazy Horse, whose name means "untamed horse" rather than "insane horse." At thirty-two, he was a quiet, generous man wise in the ways of war. All agreed that he was the bravest of the brave. No warrior could get ahead of him in attacking an enemy. Victorious, he gave his loot away to the poor, keeping nothing but weapons for himself. When game was scarce, he refused to eat while any of his people went hungry.

Crazy Horse waited behind a hill with a thousand mounted warriors as Crook's force, numbering also about a thousand, marched along the Rosebud. Although a great chief with many coups, he wore no feather bonnet, only a hawk feather pinned to his long black hair. A lightning bolt was

Crazy Horse.
Although pictured on a 1982
postage stamp, no photograph
was ever made of the great
Oglala war chief. No one
today can say what he looked
like. For the first time the
United States has honored an
enemy leader who defeated its
army in war.

painted across his face, and dots representing hailstones marked his body.

As the troops drew near, Crazy Horse threw a handful of dust over himself and his horse for good luck. His war cry shattered the quiet of the day. "*Hookahey!* Come on, Dakotas, it's a good day to die!"

Crazy Horse showed his braves how to fight in ways they never imagined. Instead of charging head-on, he had a wave of horsemen break to the right and left, striking the soldiers' flanks, the unprotected sides of their formation. He kept his men mounted, darting and hitting like a boxer whenever the enemy lowered his guard for a moment.

Both sides fought courageously, although the Indians agreed that a Cheyenne was bravest of all. Chief Comes-in-Sight was swinging his horse away after an attack when a bullet brought it down in front of a line of footsoldiers. Bullets whined, kicking up the dust all around him. Some of General Crook's Crow scouts were running toward him when a horse and rider dashed between them. A hand reached down and in a second the chief was behind the rider, galloping to safety. He had been rescued by his sister, Buffalo-Calf-Road-Woman, as good a rider as any warrior. That's why the Indians called the fight the Battle Where the Girl Saved Her Brother.

The Army called it the Battle of the Rosebud, claiming a victory because the Indians finally pulled back. But the soldiers who fought there knew better; for they'd been whipped fair and square. Crook buried his dead, retreated to safety, and rested his battered troops. A few days later, when Sitting Bull moved his camp, they were still not recovered enough to follow. The Sioux's new campsite lay to the west, over the next ridgeline, along the banks of the Little Bighorn River.

In the meantime, General Terry and Colonel Gibbon had joined forces on the Yellowstone. The backbone of the general's command was the Seventh Cavalry under Colonel Custer, one of the nation's most famous soldiers. We have already met Custer, and must now get to know him better.

George Armstrong Custer was born December 5, 1839, in New Rumley, Ohio. He was never very good at schoolwork, and when he graduated from the United States Military Academy at West Point it was as the lowest man in his class. Not that being low man really mattered, for the year was 1861 and the Civil War was in full swing. The army needed men, and he rushed to ask for a battlefield command. Custer quickly proved himself a daredevil cavalry commander, rising in four years from the rank of lieutenant to major general. The "Boy General" they called him, for he was only twenty-four. When the war ended, Custer had to give up his general's rank and become a colonel in order to remain in the service.

You'd never miss Custer in a crowd. A six-footer, weighing one hundred seventy pounds, he had blue eyes and golden-brown hair. The Indians called him Pe-hin Hanska—Long Hair—because he wore his hair shoulder length. His men called him "Old Curly."

The "Boy General." George Armstrong Custer became a major general at the age of twenty-four during the Civil War. After the war, he took the rank of lieutenant colonel in order to remain in the Army.

Custer was a flashy dresser who invented his own frontier costume rather than wear the standard army uniform. He wore blue flannel pants and a shirt to match. His jacket was buckskin with fringes dangling from the sleeves. A red bandanna was knotted around his neck and he wore a broad-brimmed sombrero to keep the sun out of his eyes.

Custer was high-spirited and never hid his feelings. Everyone knew exactly how he felt at any time. When he was sad, he sulked, but when he was happy, he went wild with joy. He'd run around his quarters whooping and yelling at the top of his voice as he smashed the furniture to splinters. He'd toss his wife, Elizabeth ("Libby"), into the air, laughing as tears ran down his cheeks.

The couple was deeply in love, and he couldn't stand being away from her for any length of time. She went with him most places, riding at his side on a spirited cavalry horse. Once Custer and Libby were crossing the Plains at the head of the Seventh Cavalry when she felt an arm lock around her waist. Her husband lifted her out of the saddle, held her high in the air for a moment, and gently put her back in the saddle without saying a word. When they had to be separated, he wrote her every night—thirty-two page letters. The gallant soldier called his wife "Dear Little Durl," "My Rosebud," and "Little Army Crow." And to her he was always "Beloved Star" and "My Darling Boy."

Custer also loved animals, any animal he could ride or pet or talk to, including a bobcat, porcupine, and wild turkey. He had a pack of twenty to thirty hunting dogs, which he took along during campaigns and allowed to share his bed at night. He even captured and tamed a field mouse. During quiet moments, he took it out of the empty ink bottle on his desk and taught it tricks. After Libby made him let it go, it kept coming back to renew its friendship with the soldier.

Yet there was another, less pleasant, side to Custer. He never stopped talking about his accomplishments and how wonderful he was. Anyone who disagreed with him or couldn't do things his way received a tongue lashing. The colonel's dressing downs embarrassed people, who bore him a grudge from then on. They obeyed his orders, like good soldiers, but had no liking for the man.

Custer always remained a big boy who never completely grew up. General Sherman said he was "very brave," although he "lacked sense." That lack of sense made him dangerous to himself and everyone around him. In the end it killed him and many other brave men besides.

The Seventh Cavalry had a special mission. Army scouts had found a trail a half-mile wide leading westward from the Rosebud. General Terry knew that so large a trail could only have been made by Sitting Bull's people moving to a fresh campsite along the Little Bighorn. His plan called for Colonel Gibbon's and his own troops to march up the valley of the Little Bighorn from the north. Custer would also move out, following the Rosebud until he found the Indian trail. To make sure there was no misunderstanding, Terry gave him written orders spelling out exactly what he must and mustn't do.

Custer was not—NOT, repeat, NOT—to follow the trail. Instead, he was to keep going, circle around, and come down the Little Bighorn from the south. Both columns would attack on June 26, destroying the Indians in a crossfire.

Custer had no doubt that he'd win; in fact, he knew that he and the 7th Cavalry could defeat the Indians single-handedly. "I could whip all the Indians on the Continent with the Seventh Cavalry," he boasted.

General Terry, knowing Custer's arrogance, decided to be on the safe side by offering him extra troops. Custer politely refused. He wanted all the glory for himself and his regiment. Terry then offered him three Gatling guns, an early type of machine gun. Again Custer refused, because they were too heavy and would "embarrass" him.

As the 7th Cavalry marched away, Colonel Gibbon called out: "Now, Custer, don't be greedy. Wait for us." Gibbon wasn't joking. He feared that Custer might try to take on the whole Sioux nation by himself.

Old Curly turned in the saddle, waved, and called back,

"No, I won't." What did he mean? Would he wait? Or would he do as he pleased? The answers would come soon enough.

The 7th Cavalry marched with about six hundred men, plus forty-four Crow and Arikara Indian scouts. Custer drove them hard. Day and night they rode with only short rest stops. Custer alone seemed not to mind the pace. He could go all day, have two hours sleep, and be in the saddle at dawn as fresh as ever.

Men and horses were already exhausted when the scouts found the trail on the third day, June 24. The colonel took off his sombrero and, waving it over his head, pointed west. Custer, like Fetterman, had disobeyed orders. No matter, for nobody would question him if he succeeded. And George Armstrong Custer always succeeded. Didn't he?

Night came, inky-black, with only moonlight to show the way. Some troopers were unable to see their hands in front of their eyes and had to rattle their drinking cups to keep contact. Others just leaned over, wrapped their arms around their horses' necks, and dozed off for a few minutes at a time.

Custer was as awake and talkative as ever. During a rest stop he told some Arikara scouts that victory over the Sioux would make him the Great Father—the President of the United States. If they fought well, he promised to help their people when he came to power.

At about the same moment, Sitting Bull stood on a hilltop above the Little Bighorn, which curved like a silvery ribbon in the moonlight. His hair hung loosely about his shoulders, and his body was painted in graceful patterns. Raising his hands to the sky, he cried out to the Great Spirit. "Wakan Taka, pity me. Wherever the sun, moon, earth, four winds are, there You are always. Father, save the people, I beg you. *We wish to live!* Guard us against all misfortunes and calamities. Take pity!" Then he went home to sleep, leaving behind only some small bags of tobacco tied to twigs stuck in the ground. Thus, with an offering of sweet-smelling tobacco, Sitting Bull gave thanks for his god's generosity.

In the half-light of dawn, June 25, Crow scouts saw part of Sitting Bull's encampment from a distant hilltop. Custer was overjoyed. True, he was a full day ahead a schedule and would have to fight without Terry's and Gibbon's support. He didn't care, for he felt that nothing in the world could stop him.

The colonel immediately divided the command into four sections. Captain Frederick Benteen was sent ahead with one hundred twenty-five men to investigate some low hills and attack any Indians he met along the way. Custer himself moved with two hundred eight men, together with a one hundred fifteen-man force under Major Marcus Reno. The remaining troops stayed behind with the pack mules and supplies.

Custer's actions were those of a gambler risking everything on one throw of the dice. Army officers are taught never to go after the enemy without first having a good idea of his location and strength. Custer had neither. He knew that Sitting Bull's camp lay along the Little Bighorn, but not how far it stretched. In fact, it sprawled for three miles along the riverbank and a half-mile inland, the largest encampment ever made by the Plains Indians. At its northern end lay the Cheyenne camp under Dull Knife, Two Moons and Little Wolf, experienced war chiefs. Guarding the southern end were the Hunkpapas of Sitting Bull, Gall, and Crow King. Between the two camps lay other Sioux bands: the Miniconjous of Hump, the Sans Arcs of Spotted Eagle, the Oglalas of Crazy Horse and Low Dog. Bands of Blackfeet, Brule, Two Kettle, Yankton, and Arapaho were scattered about. Santee Sioux, their memories of Minnesota still fresh, were also present. In all, as many as ten thousand Indians awaited Custer, among them at least thirty-five hundred warriors. By dividing his force, he had weakened it further, robbing it of any safety it might have had in numbers.

Custer and Reno were still several miles from the Little Bighorn when scouts reported that a group of Sioux seemed to be traveling awfully fast—in the opposite direction. A bolt of fear went through Custer. He was not afraid of fighting, but of the Indians' running away and depriving him of victory and a chance to be president. Immediately he ordered Reno to move downhill, cross the river, and charge the northern end of the encampment. He, Custer, promised to back him up with the rest of the outfit.

Reno's squadrons moved forward. Within minutes they had splashed across a shallow spot in the river and formed a battle line on the other bank. Men tightened belts and checked harness one more time. Sweaty hands patted loaded rifles and six-shooters for comfort. Their mouths went dry. Their stomachs knotted with tension. Then Reno gave the signal to advance.

Two miles to go, and the trot became a charge. A guidon, a fork-tailed flag, with a large 7 on it, snapped in the breeze. The battle was on.

The Indians were enjoying the fine summer's day. It was a happy camp, busy and filled with laughter. Women chatted as they combed the flower-covered hillsides for wild turnips. Young men slept late, after a whole night of socials, singing, and dancing. Naked children splashed in the cold river as teenage girls kept reminding them to be careful.

Black Elk, a thirteen-year-old Oglala, was watching his father's horse herd near the river. The sun was beating down hard when he left the horses with a cousin and went swimming with some friends. Suddenly the boys heard a shout from the Hunkpapa camp. "The chargers are coming! They are charging! The chargers are coming!" Looking up, Black

CRA

Indian Camp

SITTING
BULL

Medicir

GALL

Little Big Horn

RENO

Reno-Bent
Battlefiel

Ford   RENO

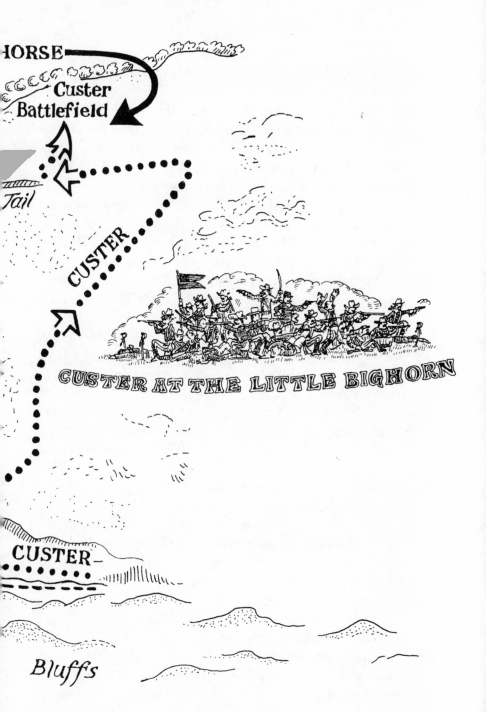

HORSE

Custer Battlefield

Tail

CUSTER

CUSTER AT THE LITTLE BIGHORN

CUSTER

Bluffs

Elk saw a pillar of dust rising in the south, where Reno was advancing.

Many others heard the alarm and saw the dust cloud. The camp became a beehive of excitement. Black Elk and his friends caught their fathers' and older brothers' warhorses. Wives held their husbands' weapons as they painted for battle. Old men shouted advice and encouragement.

Sitting Bull burst from his tipi. As warriors gathered around him, his voice boomed above the noise and confusion: "Be brave, men. It will be a hard time. Be brave!" Then he whipped his horse in the direction of the rising dust.

Sitting Bull's men were galloping ahead when a tremendous noise overtook them from behind. Crazy Horse was leading the Oglalas to battle.

The Oglalas came like lightning ripping across the prairie. Their horses' hoofs thundered, tossing up clouds of earth. Their eagle-wing-bone whistles set up a piercing, flesh-raising screech.

"Crazy Horse! Crazy Horse! Crazy Horse!" onlookers shouted as they recognized him. Their cry became a deafening roar, taken up by thousands of voices. Dogs scurried out of the way, yelping. Mothers grabbed their toddlers and dived behind the nearest tree or boulder. Tipis toppled, scattering household goods across the ground.

Crazy Horse rode his yellow pinto and was naked except for a cloth around his waist. "*Hookahey! Hookahey!*" he called to his warriors. "It is a good day to fight! It is a good day to die! Stout hearts, brave hearts, to the front! Weak hearts and cowards to the rear!"

"*Hookahey! Hookahey!* It is a good day to fight!" they cried, echoing him. No one went to the rear.

Reno's troopers knew they were in trouble. The village ahead grew larger by the second, spreading out further than the eye could see. Soon they could see nothing but dust clouds.

Braves were riding back and forth to raise a "smoke screen" until reinforcements arrived.

They arrived, charging out of the dust by the hundreds, by the thousands.

Reno's men fired from the saddle as one man, but it did no good. Except for wiping out Chief Gall's entire family in the camp ahead, the bullets couldn't stop the Indians.

Reno turned around, expecting to see Custer racing to his aid. The colonel was nowhere to be seen. Reno's detachment was alone.

The major's right hand went up, pointing to a wooded area along the river. His men dashed for the cover and, dismounting, began to fight on foot. Indian bullets whipped through the trees, showering the men below with leaves.

A soldier dropped, then another, and another. "Oh, God, I'm hit," someone screamed as he squirmed on the ground, kicking in pain. Bloody Knife, the army's chief Arikara scout, was standing next to Reno when a bullet hit him in the head. Reno, covered with the scout's blood and brains, shook all over. Struggling to control himself, he ordered a retreat across the river.

Actually, it wasn't a military retreat, neat and orderly, but an everyone-for-himself stampede. The cavalrymen remounted and headed for the riverbank as fast as their horses could carry them. But it was six feet high at their crossing point and the horses teetered at the edge, afraid to jump. Soldiers whipped their mounts with all their strength. The terrified animals jumped, but for many it didn't matter anyhow. Whooping Indians blazed away at them from the riverbank or chased them into the water. Coming alongside one trooper, a brave leaped from his horse, knocked him into the water, and held him under until he stopped struggling.

Another brave waved a blue shirt with the number seven on its collar tab. "This day my heart is made good!" he

Chief Gall, a famous Hunkpape Sioux warrior, turned back Major Reno's charge and then doubled back down the Little Bighorn River with Crazy Horse to destroy Custer's detachment.

shouted, tears rolling down his cheeks. He had lost his family on the Washita.

Half of Reno's command was dead or wounded by the time it reached the other bank. Whipping and spurring their exhausted horses uphill, the men dismounted once again. As every fourth man held the reins of the others' horses, they prepared a rough defense line. The men were bracing for a mass attack when the Indians suddenly disappeared. Except for a few braves who stayed behind to take potshots, Reno's troopers had the hill to themselves.

By easing the pressure on Reno, the Indians ended his colonel's dream of glory. Custer had good reason for not helping Reno when the battle began. The major had already gone ahead when the sound of gunfire came from the valley below. A plan began to form in Custer's mind. Instead of following Reno, he veered to the right, along the bluffs overlooking the Little Bighorn.

After a few minutes, Custer saw the whole Indian enencampment for the first time. Its size surprised him, but also made him happy. Slapping his leg with his sombrero, he called out, half-laughing, "We've got them! We've caught them napping! Come on!"

Old Curly paused just long enough to give Trooper John Martin a message scribbled on a piece of notebook paper: "Benteen. Come on. Big village. Be quick. Bring packs. P.S. Bring packs." This call for ammunition packs from the mule train was his last contact with the outside world. Trooper Martin was the last white man to see Custer's detachment alive.

The cavalrymen were galloping along the bluffs, raising a dust cloud, when they were sighted from the encampment and by warriors fighting Reno. Custer's plan was simple—and deadly. With Reno keeping most of the warriors occupied, he meant to strike the undefended encampment from across the river. Burning tipis and thousands of fleeing women and children would spread panic in the warriors' rear. The Custer luck might still hold, might still bring victory against enormous odds.

But luck, like the wind, can change at any moment. Custer's cavalrymen lined up in attack formation and began to follow Medicine Tail, a small, dry valley leading from the bluffs to the river. Already people from the camp were fleeing onto the open prairie in terror.

Credit for winning the Battle of the Little Bighorn should go to four Cheyenne warriors who had returned from hunting too late to join in the Reno fight. The names of three were Bobtail Horse, Calf, and Roan Bear. The name of the fourth man is unknown.

These four didn't flee with the others, but turned to attack. As the cavalry advanced, they crossed the river and took cover in a gully, opening fire at close range. The soldiers could easily have ridden them down, had they known their true strength. Suspecting an ambush, however, the column turned around and continued along the top of the bluffs. It was their last chance and they let it go by.

The four braves had bought precious time for their comrades downstream. The Sioux were about to crush Reno when they noticed Custer; that's why they broke off the attack so quickly. Chief Gall, heartbroken at losing his family, tore along the riverbank at the head of his warriors. Crazy Horse also rushed back, only he had to go further, for he went clear through to the northern end of the camp before crossing the river. These two groups of warriors formed the jaws of a gigantic trap with Custer in the middle.

Gall struck first. His men raced up the bluffs, shouting and shooting all the way. The soldiers fought a desperate rearguard action. Small groups dismounted, trying to cover their comrades' retreat as best they could. Courageous though they were, their courage meant nothing against the oncoming swarm. Even their own horses seemed to be against them. Each man fired from the knee for better aim, holding his horse's reins over his arm. The terrified animals reared, jerked away, and stampeded. Wounded horses whinnied in pain, frightening others so that they also broke away.

The troopers' defense collapsed. Men ran on foot, only to be shot or ridden down by tomahawk-swinging braves. Those who still had horses pushed them without mercy. The animals were exhausted, and it took a lot to keep them moving. The poor creatures reared and plunged, trampling little packets of tobacco dangling from twigs stuck into the ground.

Custer's six-shooter barked as he fought for his life and tried to command his men at the same time. A hill loomed ahead of him. That hill was hope, and life. For if the troopers could reach the hilltop and dig in, they might hold out until General Terry arrived.

Men were falling all around him, but Custer kept pointing to that hilltop and shouting for them to push on. They reached the base of the hill, riding or stumbling under a rain of arrows. Up they went, the hilltop growing larger each moment. Soon the survivors, about seventy-five men by now, would be able to form a defense line. With hearts pounding and lungs near bursting, they struggled onward.

They had nearly reached their goal when they froze in their tracks. Their hearts sank. Crazy Horse had just ridden over the crest of the hill.

Custer's "last stand" took place only a few dozen yards from safety. Clouds of dust and gunsmoke swirled around the hill, making the fighters seem like shadows rather than real people. Men coughed. Gunsmoke stung their eyes, making tears flow. Troopers shot their horses and dropped down behind the carcasses, desperate for a hiding place.

An artist's idea of what the Battle of the Little Bighorn must have been like. Crazy Horse's braves are charging from the left, while Gall's warriors advance on the right, catching the remainder of Custer's force between them.

Nothing helped. Attacked in front by Gall and in the rear by Crazy Horse, Custer's men went down under the downpour of arrows and bullets. Custer was among the last to fall, shot through the head and body.

Victorious Indians combed the hillside for anyone they might have missed during the battle. None were spared. Wounded cavalrymen were killed; some shot themselves rather than face torture. Most were scalped, although not Custer. Black Elk saw a wounded soldier kicking on the ground. "Boy, get off and scalp him," a warrior commanded. The youngster did as he was told.

Braves took the soldiers' weapons and clothing, leaving only naked bodies behind. They also found large amounts of green paper. Thinking the paper useless, they flung it into the air, laughing as it fell to the earth. Children took handfuls of the paper to decorate their toys. The cavalrymen had been paid before setting out and stuffed the cash into their pockets. Only later would the Indians learn the value of money.

In the meantime, Captain Benteen was returning from his patrol when he received Custer's message to "be quick" with the ammunition packs. Benteen was obeying orders when he ran into Reno's detachment; the mule train wandered in

The cavalry retreat. A Sioux warrior named Red Horse drew a series of colored pictures showing what he saw during the Battle of the Little Bighorn. As he remembered it, "The Sioux charged the different soldiers and drove them in confusion; these soldiers became foolish, many throwing away their guns and raising their hands, saying, 'Sioux pity us; take us prisoners.'"

an hour later. Relief had arrived just in time, for the Indians were streaming back after finishing with Custer, determined to destroy the Seventh Cavalry completely.

The troopers fought for the rest of the day from behind dead horses and saddles heaped up as a barricade. Lack of sleep and thirst caused as much suffering as enemy bullets. Men bit their lips to stay awake. Some chewed grass for the moisture. Those who tried to fill canteens from the river had a hot reception from Sioux riflemen hidden across the way.

Nightfall brought no relief. Indian watchfires circled them in a ring of orange light. Shouts and the throbbing of drums could be heard from the encampment below. Sitting Bull's people were not celebrating victory with scalp dances, but mourning the dead, their own as well as the enemy's. "My heart is full of sorrow," said Sitting Bull, "that so many were killed on either side, but when they force us to fight, we must fight. Tonight we shall mourn for our dead, and for those brave white men lying up yonder on the hillside."

Dawn brought renewed fighting. Hour after hour, the Indians charged, were thrown back, and charged again. Around noontime, just as the soldiers were beginning to lose hope, the attacks slackened off, then stopped altogether. "A trick. Be careful," the warning passed down the line. Time passed. An inquisitive fellow, growing restless, stood up. Before long the whole command ringed the edge of the hill.

No man present that day ever forgot what he saw. The valley floor seemed to be moving. Thousands of men, women, and children rode horses dragging travois upon which their belongings were tied. Other thousands of horses followed the procession, driven ahead by youngsters waving blankets. The Indians were leaving. The battle was over.

Terry and Gibbons arrived next morning, June 27, right on schedule. They were amazed at what they found. Custer's disobedience and pride had cost the Seventh Cavalry dearly.

Of its six hundred men, three hundred seventeen were dead or wounded. The Indians lost between thirty and fifty killed, plus about one hundred wounded.

Custer's defeat was the worst ever suffered by the United States Army at the Indians' hands. The army lost not only because of Custer's errors, but because the Indians fought better than anyone thought they could. Captain Benteen was right when he said, "There were a great deal too many Indians who were powerful good shots on the other side."

But good shooting doesn't tell the whole story. The Indians also won because they felt justice was on their side, and that feeling gave them strength. They had not come to fight the *Wasichus*; the *Wasichus* invaded their homeland. Benteen and other soldiers knew deep down that the Indians had not picked this fight. He said, "We were at their hearths and homes—and they were fighting for all the good God gives anyone to fight for." Truer words were never spoken.

Sitting Bull had good reasons for calling his warriors away from Reno's hill. Ammunition was running low and couldn't easily be replaced. He also knew that his people couldn't afford a total victory. It was one thing to beat Custer, another to wipe out a whole cavalry regiment. "That's enough," he cried, "let them go! If we kill them all, they will send a bigger army against us." And so the Indians broke camp and scattered, each band going its own way.

Sitting Bull had cause to worry, for the Army had sworn to avenge Custer. In the days that followed, telegraph receivers clicked out meassages in forts throughout the West. All available men and supplies were woven into a giant net to catch the Sioux and their allies.

General Terry was already on the trail, and he was soon joined by General Crook, eager to make up for his defeat on the Rosebud. Colonel Ranald Mackenzie, rawhide-tough and fresh from his conquest of the Comanches, rode up from Texas. Colonel Nelson A. Miles, a big, handsome fellow with one of the keenest minds in the Army, cheered his men with a song:

We're marching off for Sitting Bull
And this is the way we go—
Forty miles a day, on beans and hay,
In the Regular Army, O!

Colonel Wesley Merritt, one of Crook's officers, went into action first, against the northern Cheyenne. Merritt turned the tables on the Indians by deliberately sending a wagon train to be ambushed near War Bonnet Creek in southern South Dakota. The Indians took the bait and were themselves ambushed by cavalrymen hidden behind a hill.

Among the fighters that day (July 17, 1876) was Buffalo Bill Cody, Merritt's head scout. Chief Yellow Hand recognized the famous hunter and challenged him to a one-on-one fight to the death. Buffalo Bill accepted the challenge and they raced toward each other, six-shooters blazing.

The Indian's horse was hit, going down at the very moment his opponent's mount tripped over a gopher hole. Both men sprang to their feet, firing as they advanced. Buffalo Bill was the better marksman. He later told how he "scientifically scalped" Yellow Hand in five seconds. As the soldiers came up, he waved his trophy in the air shouting, "The first scalp for Custer!"

Crook hung onto the Indians' trail. Although his men were exhausted, he marched them through drenching rainstorms and an early cold snap that chilled them to the bone. Food ran low, but he kept going, noting grimly that they could eat their horses if necessary. He meant it, and they did.

Custer avenged. Buffalo Bill Cody, scout and hunter, killed and scalped the Sioux chief Yellow Hand in revenge for Custer's death.

Cavalrymen actually developed a taste for the stringy, sweat-smelling meat.

Crook's persistence paid off on September 8, 1876, in a dawn attack on a Sioux camp near Slim Buttes in northwestern South Dakota. The battle raged all morning, with the soldiers taking turns fighting and wolfing down captured pemmican. The battle seemed nearly over until Crazy Horse arrived with his braves. Their camp lay nearby and they had heard the heavy gunfire.

Crook had no intention of allowing the Oglala chief to beat him again. Although outnumbered, the troopers fought Crazy Horse to a standstill. By nightfall he had enough of fighting and withdrew. But so did Crook. With walking skeletons for horses and men dizzy with hunger, he turned toward his supply base at Deadwood in the Black Hills.

Winter brought Mackenzie's Fourth Cavalry to the Wyoming prairie. His troopers, muffled in fur and wool, rode across a white wasteland gripped by sub-zero temperatures. At dawn, November 26, 1876, he attacked the Cheyenne camp of Chief Dull Knife on the bank of the Crazy Woman Fork of the Powder River.

It was the Palo Duro all over again. Mackenzie's men drove the Indians, many of them naked, into the biting cold. Everything—food, clothing, tipis, weapons—was destroyed. The horses were shot.

The cold proved to be deadlier than bullets. As temperatures plummeted, the very young and the very old froze. Things became so bad that the few remaining horses were killed and their bodies split open. Little children were then pushed inside to be protected by the warm walls of flesh; old people were allowed to thrust their hands and feet in alongside the children.

Crook broke the power of the Northern Cheyenne in this and other raids. One band after another surrendered rather than wander the windswept plains without food or proper shelter. As quickly as they surrendered, they were sent to join their southern Cheyenne cousins on reservations in Oklahoma and in the Dakotas.

The main enemies, though, were still at large—Sitting Bull and Crazy Horse. Colonel Miles found Sitting Bull's trail in the autumn of 1876 and stayed with it no matter how fast and far his enemy moved.

Miles caught up to Sitting Bull near the Tongue River, another branch of the Yellowstone. Sitting Bull didn't want to fight, nor did he want to surrender. When he heard that "Bear Coat" Miles was nearby, he made a half-breed who had joined his band write the colonel a note. "I want to know what you are doing traveling on this road. You scare all the buffalo away. I want to hunt in this place. I want you to turn back from here. If you don't I will fight you again. I want you to leave what you have got (food and ammunition) here and turn back from here."

Miles was not a man to scare easily or back away from trouble. Instead of retreating, he sent word that he'd like to see Sitting Bull in perseon.

The leaders sat on horseback between lines of fighting men standing at either end of a clearing. It was a tense meeting. Sitting Bull began by saying that he wanted only to live in peace in his own country. Miles brushed this aside, demanding that the Hunkpapas give up and settle on a reservation.

Sitting Bull's face flushed with anger. His eyes narrowed. Proudly, defiantly, he gave his answer: "Almighty God made me an Indian—but not a reservation Indian!"

The men parted, riding back to their own lines. Fifteen minutes later, Miles gave the order to open fire. The Sioux managed to escape this time and the next two times that Miles caught up with them. But Sitting Bull grew tired of running. Victory over Custer hadn't brought peace, only everlasting war. He wanted a safe place where his people could sleep without fear of gunfire waking them in the chill dawn. Early in 1877, he led the Hunkpapas across the border to exile in Canada.

Only Crazy Horse and the Oglalas remained. Miles set

out after him with only four hundred thirty-two men and two hidden "equalizers." His troopers had to make way through knee-deep snow, but finally caught up to the Oglalas on January 1, 1877.

Yet it seemed that Crazy Horse had really caught up with Miles. Over a thousand mounted braves lined a hilltop to open fire on the soldiers below. There was no point in taking cover, since the enemy held the high ground. There was only one thing to do: the soldiers charged up the hill on foot, wading through snow drifts all the way. At the same time, two wagons turned out of line. Soldiers stripped off their canvas covers to reveal two light cannon. Within minutes bursting shells were raking the hilltop.

Miles kept up the pressure during the weeks that followed, forcing the Oglala bands to give up one at a time. Finally Crazy Horse himself surrendered. On September 5, 1877, a soldier bayoneted him when he refused to be locked in a guardhouse. Crazy Horse's parents rode off with his body the next day. Some say he is buried along a creek called Wounded Knee. We'll never know because the old couple never revealed his resting place.

That autumn of 1877 was a turning point. Within a year of their greatest victory, the Sioux and Cheyenne lost everything they had fought for. From Canada south to the Mexican border, from the Mississippi River westward to the slopes of the Rockies, no Indian tribe roamed freely or would ever again roam freely over the Great Plains.

five

The Long March of the Nez Percé

Old Joseph, they called their beloved chief. He was a man of many winters, but this winter of 1871 was to be his last. He lay in his tipi quietly, unafraid, waiting for the end.

"Where is my son?" he asked, his voice barely rising above a whisper.

A figure stepped from the shadows. Tall, standing straight as a pine tree, he wore buckskin pants and beaded moccasins; a brightly colored blanket was wrapped around his shoulders. His name was In-mut-too-yah-lat-lat. It meant Thunder Traveling Over the Mountains From the Sea, although most people simply called him Young Joseph.

He bent close, his ear almost touching his father's lips. "My son," said the chief, "my body is returning to my mother earth, and my spirit is going very soon to see the Great Spirit Chief. When I am gone, think of your country. You are the chief of these people. They look to you to guide them. Always remember that your father never sold his country."

The son held his father's hand. How strong that hand

Chief Joseph of the Nez Percés fought off thousands of United States Army troops in an effort to escape with his people to Canada.

had seemed when, as a boy, he had taught him to use the bow and arrow, and how weak it was now. Yes, the son would protect their country with his life. Old Joseph smiled, then passed away to the spirit land. Young Joseph had become chief at the age of thirty-one.

Joseph led a band of Nez Percé Indians, a name meaning "pierced noses," because of their custom of wearing rings through the nose as ornaments. The Nez Percé lived in the area where Oregon, Idaho, and Washington state meet. The land here is mountainous, cut by deep valleys carved by swiftly moving rivers such as the Salmon, Snake, and Clearwater.

Nez Percé country was not especially rich, although it gave the small bands that made up the tribe a comfortable living. The Indians cultivated vegetable gardens, hunted deer, and caught the fat salmon that swarmed in the rivers. Horse herds and cattle grazed on the lush grass near the Indian encampments. Young men crossed the mountains every summer to join their Crow friends in the buffalo hunts on the plains of Montana.

As far back as anyone could remember, the Nez Percé had been friendly to white people. The explorers Lewis and Clark met the tribe during their expedition to the Pacific in 1805 and spoke of the people as being warm, generous, and helpful. Traders found them to be sharp bargainers interested in useful things rather than colorful trinkets. The Nez Percé prided themselves on never having killed or broken a promise to a white person.

The tribe was not one large community living in the same place, but made up of several small bands led by their own chiefs. The United States Government was able to convince some chiefs to give up their land and move their people to Lapwai Reservation in Idaho. These reservation dwellers were known as the Upper Nez Percé, because they came from the upper, or northern, section of the tribal territory. Joseph's people were the lower, or southern, Nez Percé. They lived in the valley of the Wallowa River—the Land of the Winding Waters. When Old Joseph was asked to sign a treaty giving away the Wallowa, he told the agents that he was an honest man who wouldn't touch such a paper. And neither would his son.

But white settlers wanted the Land of the Winding Waters, and their government agreed that they should have it. The government saw no difficulty in getting the Indians to leave. The Sioux had just been defeated, which encouraged the belief that the Nez Percé, so few and so peaceful, wouldn't dare risk a fight with the army. That belief was mistaken.

Brigadier General Oliver Otis Howard was sent to break the news to Joseph in the spring of 1877. Howard was a Civil War hero who had lost an arm while leading a cavalry charge. A deeply religious man, he believed it his Christian duty to help the less fortunate. Howard University in Washington, D.C., is named for him and was started to help freed slaves get a college education. The Apache Indians also thought of him as a friend.

Howard, nicknamed "The Praying General," was a good man with a bad job to do. Given his own way, he would have left the Nez Percé alone; indeed, he wrote the War Department that they were "really peaceable" and that it would be a mistake to take away their lands. Still, even generals must obey orders whether they agree with them or not.

Howard told Joseph that his people no longer owned the Wallowa and must move to the reservation. Joseph replied that his people had never sold their lands and that the government had no right to ask them to move. The general became embarrassed and impatient. Joseph, he knew, was right, although that couldn't change the orders in his pocket. Thirty days: that's all the time he'd give the Indians to gather their belongings and get out. Thirty days: if they weren't out on time, the soldiers would drive them out.

Joseph was heartbroken, torn between respect for his father's memory and duty toward his people. He had promised the dying man never to give up the Wallowa. If he went back

General Oliver O. Howard lost an arm while leading a cavalry charge during the Civil War. He went on to command troops against the Nez Percé and Apaches.

on his word he'd become a liar in his own eyes. But he also had a responsibility to the living. They looked to him, needed him, depended upon him to do the right thing for them.

Joseph decided that, rather than have a war, he'd give up his country. He'd give up his father's grave. "I would give up everything," he said, "rather than have the blood of white men upon the hands of my people." The decision hurt, but it was the only thing he could do.

Some of the younger men stormed and raged, calling their chief a coward. Even so, his younger brother, Ollokot, stood by him. Ollokot was a brave man, respected even by the hotheads. At last the tribal council agreed and the Indians prepared to leave the Wallowa.

Six months' work was crowded into one as the Nez Percé packed their belongings and gathered their livestock. In their haste to meet the deadline, they overlooked many animals, which settlers took and branded as their own. The Snake River was in flood at this time and hundreds of horses and cattle were swept away when the Inidans forced them to swim across.

Joseph's band stopped to rest on the other side of the Snake River and to wait for other bands to join them before going on to the reservation. Looking Glass, White Bird, and Too-hool-hool-zote brought their people to the encampment during the next few days. Too-hool-hool-zote was not only a chief, but a respected medicine man. His name meant "Sound," because he had a deep, booming voice.

Although Joseph wanted peace, three of his braves had other ideas. The father of one had been shot by a settler the year before; another had been whipped by settlers. One night, when Joseph was away, they stole out of camp, returning in the morning with news that they had killed four whites. Again they set out, this time with a sixteen-man war party, and continued to raid and kill whites for the next two days.

Joseph must have felt like Little Crow when his Santee went on a rampage fifteen years before. His braves had started something they couldn't finish. The settlers, he knew, would demand revenge—revenge upon all Nez Percé, not just upon the guilty ones. In a day or two at the most, maybe even in a few hours, troops would be coming after them.

Joseph had to make another painful decision. Either he went with his people, leading them in war, or he left them and went to live on the reservation with his family. He chose to go with them no matter what happened.

Yet Joseph was no Little Crow, much less a Crazy Horse. Having grown up in a peaceful tribe, he knew nothing about fighting battles. He had never even *seen* a battle. Still, this man of peace became one of the greatest Indian war leaders of all time. The responsibility of leading his people in war taught Joseph many things he'd never known about himself. War was a testing time, when he was forced to think in unfamiliar ways in order to survive. "The Great Spirit," he later explained, "puts into the heart and head of man how to defend himself."

Joseph fought a different kind of war, one that surprised the army and won its commanders' respect. Unlike the Plains tribes, the Nez Percé had no love of fighting. No one, not even the worst Indian hater could accuse them of fighting like "savages." Joseph forbade harming anyone who hadn't tried to harm an Indian first. This meant that settlers, their women and children, were left alone. The Nez Percé never kidnapped people, never tortured prisoners, never scalped enemies.

Joseph discovered that he had a natural talent for warfare. Under his command, the Nez Percé never went in for hit-and-run "Indian-style" fighting. He observed the soldiers' methods of fighting, then borrowed their best tactics. He taught his braves to use advance and rear guards, and to fight from rifle pits, or fox holes, as we call them today.

The chief made full use of his people's skills. The Nez Percé were as good horsemen as any of the Plains tribes, including the Comanche. As marksmen, they were better than other Indians and, indeed, most of the soldiers they faced.

The Nez Percé learned one trick army officers didn't like. While other Indians shot at any Bluecoat who crossed their sights, the Nez Percé concentrated their fire on officers. Joseph made it his business to learn the meaning of army insignia. He then taught his men that someone with silver bars or eagles on his shoulder was more important than a soldier with three stripes on his sleeve, and to send more bullets his way.

Joseph's abilities were soon put to the test. The Nez Percé were camped in White Bird Canyon when General Howard caught up to them on June 17, 1877. Although his four hundred troopers outnumbered the Nez Percé by two to one, the Indians had the advantage of surprise. Except for the distant wail of a coyote, all was quiet as the troopers rode into the canyon. That "coyote" should have put them on guard, for imitating animal sounds was one of the Indians' favorite ways of signaling.

Joseph's lookouts were, in fact, telling their friends to close the trap. As the soldiers came in range, the Indians opened fire from the right side of the canyon and the surrounding cliffs. The soldiers retreated, leaving thirty-seven bodies behind. When the victorious Joseph returned to camp, he was greeted with the news that his wife had given birth to a son during the battle.

The Nez Percé couldn't take time out to rest after their victory. Howard, they knew, would never let them go unpunished. They would have to keep moving.

Keep moving: it was easier said than done. In addition to two hundred fifty warriors, Joseph was responsible for four hundred fifty women and children, sick and aged, plus a herd of two thousand horses. He was able to move them along quickly because everyone had a job to do and did it without complaining. Even the little children pitched in. Teamwork, the feeling that they were together in something important, allowed the Nez Percé to overcome every obstacle.

Howard, aided by Nez Percé scouts, clung to the fugitives' trail. Men from the Upper Nez Percé bands helped the general against their "outlaw" cousins. Other detachments that joined the chase were guided by Sioux and Cheyenne scouts. The fact that these tribes had just been defeated by the army didn't prevent some of their young men from siding with their ex-enemies. The army paid well, and these men had families to support. Besides, the Nez Percé were friends of the Crow, their age-old enemies.

On July 11, 1877, Joseph turned on his pursuers near the Clearwater River. Instead of attacking, he had his braves dig in and make the soldiers come to them.

They came, and learned some harsh lessons at the hands of the Nez Percé. Accurate rifle fire forced them to dismount and take cover as best they could. An officer raised his hand for a second and had a neat hole drilled through his wrist. A thirsty private lay on his back and tilted his canteen to get the last drops of water. He felt a strange tugging, then his face was wet; a bullet had cut off the canteen's neck as he held it to his lips. Once again the soldiers had to give up the chase for a while.

The Clearwater fight made Joseph realize that this routine of fighting and running couldn't go on forever. Sooner or later there wouldn't be any Indians left to fight and run. There was only one thing to do. The Nez Percé would have to follow Sitting Bull's people into exile in Canada.

Sitting Bull's retreat was easy, compared to what the Nez Percé faced. A handful of braves would have to stand off thousands of soldiers. The people would have to keep ahead of their pursuers, crossing broad rivers and rugged mountain ranges. Joseph called his braves together and reminded them of how they had accused him of being afraid of whites. "Stay with me now and you shall have your bellies well filled with fighting." Rifles held high, they cheered their leader. They'd follow him anywhere.

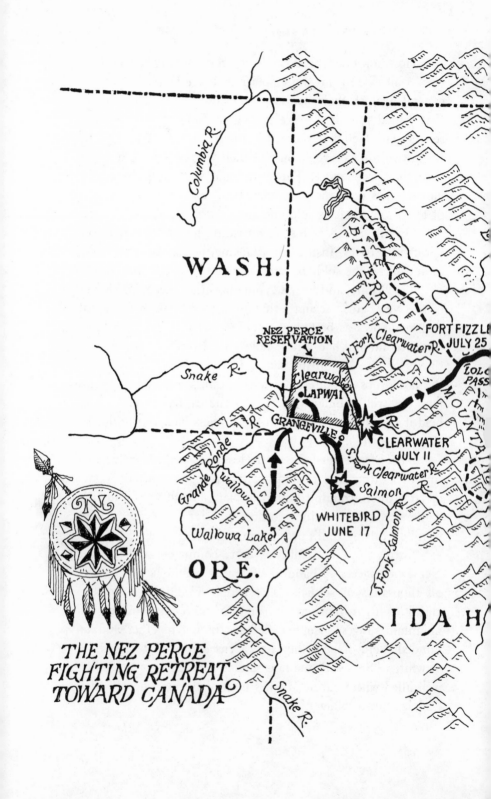

THE NEZ PERCE
FIGHTING RETREAT
TOWARD CANADA

WASH.

ORE.

IDAHO

Columbia R.

Snake R.

NEZ PERCE
RESERVATION

Clearwater

LAPWAI

GRANDEVILLE

Grande Ronde R.

Wallowa

Wallowa Lake

N. Fork Clearwater R.

BITTERROOT

FORT FIZZLE
JULY 25

LOLO
PASS

MOUNTAINS

CLEARWATER
JULY 11

S. Fork Clearwater R.

Salmon

S. Fork Salmon R.

WHITEBIRD
JUNE 17

Snake R.

ANADA
Milk R.
SURRENDER
OCTOBER 5
BEAR PAW
MTS.
COW ISLAND
SEPTEMBER 23
Fort Benton
Missouri R.
COLONEL MILES
ROUTE
MONTANA
Missoula
HELENA
Musselshell R.
CANYON CREEK
SEPTEMBER 13
BILLINGS
Big Hole R.
BIG HOLE
AUGUST 9
Yellowstone R.
Madison R.
Clark's Fork
TARGHEE PASS
YELLOWSTONE
NATIONAL PARK
CAMAS CREEK
AUGUST 20
WYOMING

Their escape route lay along the Lolo Trail across the Bitterroot Range, a branch of the Rocky Mountains chain. Once across the Bitterroots, they'd move southward into Montana, then northward to the "Grandmother's Land," as Indians called Canada because it belong to Queen Victoria of England.

The Lolo is one of the hardest trails in America. Steep and winding, it is clogged with huge boulders and fallen trees. Its shoulders, windblown and slippery, jut out over steep cliffs. A false step would send a horse and rider tumbling hundreds of feet to the rocks below. The Nez Percé were familiar with the Lolo Trail from their trips to the buffalo country and had no trouble staying two or three days ahead of Howard. The army column moved at a snail's pace, led by an advance guard of axemen to break up the log jams on the trail.

As Joseph's people neared the top of Lolo Pass, they noticed soldiers ahead of them. A sixty-man unit under Captain Charles Rawn had built a small fort across the trail.

The Nez Percé chiefs decided it was better to talk than fight; as long as the soldiers held their fire, their braves wouldn't provoke a battle. Joseph, Looking Glass, and White Bird rode calmly up to the fort for a powwow. Joseph told the captain that they would go past the troops without fighting, if he'd let them, but they'd go past no matter what happened. When they came to the lowlands, he added, they'd pass through peacefully, without harming settlers or their property.

Captain Rawn replied that they'd have to hand over their weapons if they wanted to go by. The chiefs refused; they no longer trusted army officers and wouldn't give up the only things that put both sides on an equal footing. As snipers kept the soldiers pinned down, the rest of the tribe slipped around the fort by a hidden trail. From then on the place was known as "Fort Fizzle."

Montana settlers were at first worried about the gun-toting Nez Percé braves. But when they saw that Joseph would keep his word and leave them alone, they actually helped the Indians. Shopkeepers unlocked their doors and sold them anything they needed, including rifles and ammunition. Only one shopkeeper wouldn't cooperate. He slammed his door in the Indians' faces, and they simply took their business across the street. The only thing Joseph wouldn't let his people buy was whiskey.

Joseph now made a serious mistake. Knowing that Howard was several days behind, and pleased with the settlers' friendliness, he thought his people were out of danger. For the first time, and the last, he failed to post guards. The Nez Percé camp was wide open.

The danger came not from behind, but lay in front of the Indians. Messages over the "whispering wires"—the telegraph—had ordered Colonel John Gibbon from Helena, Montana, with two hundred cavalrymen and two cannon. Toward evening, August 8, 1877, Gibbon's scouts located the sleeping camp nestled between some low, wooded hills near the Big Hole River. Gibbon, who never forgot what he had seen along the Little Bighorn the year before, snapped an order: "No prisoners!"

The dawn attack exploded like a thunderclap. Cavalrymen splashed across the shallow river and rode up the opposite bank. The Nez Percé rushed from their tipis into a hail of bullets. Many fell, but many others dived into the brush along the riverbank or ran to the high ground for cover. Within twenty minutes Gibbon had captured the village and was destroying it.

It was now the soldiers' turn to be surprised. Indians had always fled in panic when their villages were attacked, and that's what they were expected to do again. They didn't. Joseph and the other chiefs rallied them as any officer would have done. White Bird shouted, "Why are we running? Since the world was made, brave men have fought for their women and children! Fight! Shoot them down! We can shoot as well as any of these soldiers!"

No, they could shoot *better*. Nez Percé warriors sprang forward with such determination that they retook the village. It was the soldiers' turn to run. They ran, fast, to the top of a nearby hill and dug in as best they could.

Joseph's sharpshooters aimed carefully, squeezing off one shot at a time. Few bullets failed to find their mark. Gibbon later wrote that a soldier was sure to fall nearly every time a Nez Percé rifle went off. The colonel himself took a bullet in the leg.

Yet the soldiers were far from finished. A cannon crew was racing to the hilltop as fast as its horses could pull the heavy weapon. Joseph, however, saw what was happening and sent thirty braves to cut them off. The gun crew panicked as the braves drew near. "This is another Custer massacre" someone shouted, sending his comrades running for cover. Luckily for the soldiers, the warriors didn't know how to operate cannon, otherwise they would have been in far worse trouble. The Indians had to be satisfied with disabling the cannon so it couldn't be used against them.

The battle raged all day. Late in the afternoon, as the soldiers were beginning to feel a little safer, the breeze brought an unusual odor—smoke. The Indians had set a grass fire and the wind was blowing a wall of flame toward their dugouts. If it reached them, driving them from cover, they'd be shot like jackrabbits. Again, their luck held, for the wind shifted, blowing the fire back on its own ashes and putting it out. The soldiers cheered.

Night made them feel more like moaning than cheering. Their canteens were empty and they had no food, except for a dead horse that had begun to stink. They dared not light cooking fires for fear of snipers, so they ate the animal raw.

Joseph wasn't interested in wiping out Gibbon's detachment. During the next two days the women and children broke camp and slipped away while the warriors kept the soldiers busy. When they were in the clear, the warriors, too, faded away, leaving the colonel to count his blessings.

Joseph had turned defeat into victory, yet it was a costly victory. The Nez Percé counted eighty-nine killed, of which fifty were women and children mowed down in the first minutes of fighting. Gibbon had twenty-nine killed and forty wounded. Neither side had reason to be happy.

Big Hole taught Joseph to be doubly careful in the future. He posted scouts far back on the trail to keep tabs on General Howard's movements. One day they reported that a troop of cavalry—forty-five men and an officer—had ridden out of Howard's camp on a mission. Here was a golden opportunity to turn the tables on "One-Arm" Howard.

On the night of August 20, 1877, a guard was making his rounds outside the soldiers' camp when he heard hoofbeats. Coming toward him in the moonlight was a column of horsemen. The cavalry troop was returning, he thought.

It wasn't. Joseph's braves rode right into the camp in cavalry formation and opened fire. Troopers tumbled out of their bed rolls and, recovering from their surprise, saddled up and went after the raiders—right into an ambush. Joseph knew he'd be chased and set a trap for the pursuers. The cavalrymen suddenly saw orange flames cut the darkness ahead and on either side of them. They retreated. When the smoke cleared, Howard found himself minus a few troopers and all of his pack mules. And since his men couldn't carry tons of supplies and ammunition on their backs, he had to halt until fresh animals arrived. Joseph's quick thinking had given his people a three-day headstart.

Onward, always onward, the Indians trudged, never slowing the pace. Hundreds of horses dropped from overwork, but there were always others to take their place. The people, too, were exhausted, but they kept going. There was always another ridgeline to cross, always another river to ford.

After coming through the mountains at Targhee Pass, they followed the trail across Yellowstone National Park and crossed the curving Yellowstone River twice. Small cavalry units barred the way across the Musselshell and Missouri Rivers, but Joseph's veterans easily brushed them aside.

In the distance loomed the Bear Paw Mountains. Nez Percé hearts leaped for joy, because Grandmother's land and safety lay a mere thirty miles to the north.

A day's march brought them to the Bear Paws, where they rested. His people were so exhausted by now, and their pursuers left so far behind, that Joesph saw no harm in stopping. They'd rest a day or two, then push on to Canada, less than a day's march away.

But General Howard was not one to give up once he decided to do something. After replacing his pack mules and tending to the wounded, he pushed his column as fast as it could go. His troops, he knew, would never catch the Nez Percé unless something slowed them down. Again the whispering wires carried messages, this time to Colonel Miles at Fort Keogh, Wyoming. Miles set out with cavalry, mounted infantry, cannon, and a long train of supply wagons. His force arrived at the Nez Percé camp to block Joseph's path on October 2, 1877.

The Indian camp lay in a hollow surrounded by cliffs on three sides. At daybreak, lookouts on the cliffs began waving brightly colored blankets to signal danger. The ground shook with the hoofbeats of six hundred charging horses.

At the first warning, Joseph's braves took positions in front of the camp. Although outnumbered four to one, they met the charge with a sheet of flame and smoke. One in four

Nelson A. Miles as a brigadier general. It was Miles who finally trapped Joseph's Nez Percés when they were within reach of the Canadian border.

soldiers toppled from the saddle during the first minutes of fighting. Even so, they succeeded in cutting the Nez Percé camp in half, capturing nearly all the horses.

Joseph was on the other side of the camp with his twelve-year-old daughter when the soldiers came. As soon as the shooting began, he put her on a horse and told her to get away from the area as fast as she could. The chief then jerked his own horse's bridle, turning it toward the battle.

Joseph's mouth moved in prayer as he galloped, unarmed, through the swarm of cavalrymen to join his people. Bullets grazed his horse. Bullets slashed his clothes. Still he rode on, unhurt, until he stopped at the door of his tipi. His wife stood there with his rifle in her hand. "Here's your gun," she cried. "Fight!"

He fought harder than he had ever fought before. Slowly, under a hail of bullets, he pulled his people back to the nearby hillside, where they dug in. While the warriors fought, the women and children used everything—shovels, knives, frying pans, bare hands—to dig those lifesaving holes.

Colonel Miles saw that he had a tiger by the tail. He didn't dare keep up head-on attacks without destroying his own force. The only thing to do was to bring up his cannon and wait for General Howard to arrive with reinforcements.

Cannon and rifles, cold and hunger, did their work for three days. Ollokot was killed, then Looking Glass and Too-hool-hool-zote. Joseph mourned as if they were all his brothers.

The Nez Percé were trapped. They knew it, and the soldiers knew it, too. Toward sunset, October 5, 1877, a white flag fluttered above the Indians' position. Six men came forward, five walking, one on horseback—Joseph.

His body was bent forward, his head was bowed, and his hands were folded over the saddle horn.

General Howard and Colonel Miles stood waiting at the foot of a small hill. Joseph stopped, said something to his escorts, and went on to meet the officers alone.

As he dismounted, they noticed bullet scars on his cheeks and wrists. Bullet holes riddled the gray blanket draped across his shoulders. Joseph handed his rifle to Miles, butt first, as a sign of surrender. Then he spoke, as an interpreter translated his words into English.

His words were to become the most famous of all American Indian speeches.

Tell General Howard that I know his heart. What he told me before I have in my heart. I am tired of fighting. Our chiefs are killed. Looking Glass is dead. The old men are all dead. It is the young men now, who say 'yes' or 'no.' He who led the young men (the chief couldn't bear to name his slain brother, Ollokot) is dead. It is cold, and we have no blankets. The little children are freezing to death. My people—some of them—have run away to the hills, and we have no blankets, no food. No one knows where they are—perhaps freezing to death. I want to have time to look for my children,* and see how many of them I can find; maybe I shall find them among the dead. Hear me, my chiefs, my heart is sick and sad. From where the sun now stands, I will fight no more forever.

When he finished, Joseph drew the corner of his blanket across his face, as Indians did when in mourning or humiliated. Then, instead of returning to his people, he walked into the Army camp as a prisoner. The Nez Percé rose from their dugouts and followed.

Joseph had nothing to be ashamed of. Colonel Miles, who defeated him, gave him a soldier's tribute. "Chief Joseph was the highest type of Indian I have ever known, very handsome, kind, and brave." Miles, like Captain Benteen, added that the Indians had been wronged by the settlers and the government.

* Joseph's six children were found safe; White Bird took his twelve-year-old daughter to Canada, where they were given shelter by Sitting Bull's people.

Joseph had led his people on a two-thousand-mile march through enemy territory, taking his wounded and women and children with him. Although he had fewer than three hundred warriors, he met over two thousand of the United States Army's best soldiers in battle, while another three thousand stood by as reserves. He fought thirteen battles, winning them all except the last. The fighting cost the Nez Percé two hundred thirty-nine killed and wounded; the army lost two hundred sixty-six killed and wounded.

The Nez Percé war ended, but the sufferings of the Nez Percé people were just beginning. Colonel Miles had promised Joseph that he'd send his people to the Lapwai Reservation; it wasn't their home country, but at least it was close enough that they wouldn't feel cut off from everything they knew and loved.

Nez Percé braves mounted and in full dress some years later. In their battles with the United States Army, they never once scalped the dead or tortured prisoners

Unfortunately, government officials had other plans and quickly broke the colonel's word. Miles protested, only to find that it was like arguing with a row of stone statues. The Nez Percé were packed into railroad cars and shipped to Oklahoma. There, in a hot, dusty country so different from their mountains, many sickened and died, among them Joseph's children. Their horses and other belongings were never returned.

The best that Miles and other sympathetic whites could do was to win permission for a handful of sick and aged Indians to be sent to Lapwai in 1884. Joseph and the others were sent to Colville Reservation in Washington state the following year.

Joseph begged the authorities to let his people return to their Land of the Winding Waters. "Let me be a free man—

free to travel, free to stop, free to work, free to trade where I choose, free to choose my own teachers, free to follow the religion of my fathers, free to think and talk and act for myself—and I will obey every law, or submit to the penalty."

This was not to be. Never again would he know the freedom he longed for. The years rolled by and he was allowed to visit his homeland only once. Indian Inspector James McLaughlin took him on a short, sad journey in 1900 to show him why it was impossible for him to return.

The land was as beautiful as ever, although it had changed. Houses dotted the landscape where tipis had stood. Fences cut up the fields, yellow and red with apple orchards. Towns stood along the banks of the Wallowa River, with irrigation ditches leading to the fields. "It is still our land. We never gave it away or sold it. It is ours," the old man said, his voice cracking.

Inspector McLaughlin took him to see his father's grave. He didn't know what to expect, maybe just a hole torn by angry settlers. It was now on a white man's farm. The farmer, a decent man, had enclosed the grave with a neat picket fence and kept it clear of weeds. Tears streamed down Joseph's face as he turned to leave. He knew he'd never pass this way again.

Joseph grew sadder and spent most of the time seated before his tipi fire, brooding. So he sat when, on September 21, 1904, he suddenly pitched forward.

The reservation doctor reported the cause of death as "a broken heart."

six

Apache Means Enemy

It is a marvelous place, wild and beautiful, this Land of the Enemies. The Rocky Mountains reach into Arizona and New Mexico not as a solid wall soaring skyward, but like the spread-out fingers of a hand. The area between these stony fingers is flat, although crisscrossed in places by deep canyons. Millions of years ago, before people lived in the New World, rushing waters dug these canyons in the rock. The Pecos, Gila, and Rio Grande Rivers flow today; the Colorado dug (and still digs) the Grand Canyon, the largest and deepest crack in the earth's surface. Most of the other rivers, though, have long since dried up.

The land between these ancient river beds stands above the canyon bottoms like stone tables. These tables, or *"mesas,"* as the Spanish explorers called them, come in different sizes. Some are as big as a dining room table, while others cover hundreds of square miles. Windblown sand and rain have carved these mesas into strange shapes: towers, chimneys, arches, temples, stone "faces." Their colors are dazzling, almost blinding. Reds, yellows, and oranges blaze in the sunlight against the cloudless blue sky.

The higher mountains are snowcapped much of the year.

The cold streams that flow from them water forests of pine, spruce, and cedar. But the lower down you go, the fewer trees you find, for the mountains are so high that they prevent most rainclouds from passing over their peaks.

The lowlands are desert, studded with bare, rugged hills and sunbaked sand dunes. Summer temperatures of 110 degrees are normal, soaring to 125-130 degrees on the floors of the deeper canyons. Heatwaves shimmer, making distant mesas seem to move and creating mirages, sandy areas that look like pools of water from the distance. Trees can't live in such heat and dryness, only cactus, of which there are hundreds of types. Clumps of golden cholla (choy-ah) and pricklypear are everywhere. The saguaro, the Goliath of cacti, grows to fifty feet high and weighs ten tons.

The desert swarms with life, if you know where to look for it. By day only hawks can be seen gliding in the cool air high above. Nighttime brings the desert creatures out of their cozy burrows and from beneath stones. Nights are cool, because the temperature can drop fifty degrees after sunset. Jackrabbits and mice scurry about, and owls leave their holes in saguaro cactus to hunt them. Hairy tarantula spiders as large as the palm of your hand prowl the sands, as do deadly scorpions. Sidewinders—rattlesnakes—glide over the loose sand by throwing the loops of their body forward. Fat gila monster lizards, also poisonous, stalk smaller lizards. Coyotes howl at the moon. Their sad sound can be heard for miles.

People have lived here for thousands of years. The Hopi, Zuñi, and Pueblo Indians became expert at dry-farming, raising crops with only a little water. Skillful engineers, they built homes and fortresses of adobe, wet clay mixed with straw and baked in the sun to form bricks. Some of their villages can still be seen nestled in the walls of steep-sided mesas.

The peaceful farmers built their villages high up to pro-

*Apaches beg the mountain gods for success in hunting and war.
The Apaches lived in a harsh, dry country where only the strongest
survived.*

tect them from their neighbors. These neighbors called themselves *Inde*—The People. The farmers called them *Apache*—
The Enemy. The name stuck, and that's how they've been
known ever since. Apache means enemy.

Since the land couldn't support many people in one
place, the Apache had to spread out, wandering in small
bands named for the area in which they lived. Among these
bands were the White Mountain, Chiricahua (Chee-ree-kah-
wah), Mescalero, Jicarilla (Hee-car-eeya), and Mimbres or
Copper Mine Apaches. One band grew so large that it became
a separate tribe, the Navajo. Unlike other Apaches, the Navajo
cultivated fields of corn and melons and raised herds of cattle

and sheep in the Canyon de Chelly (Shay-ee) in northeastern Arizona.

Apaches lived by hunting small animals and gathering wild seeds. And by thievery. They never thought of stealing as wrong, but as a necessary way of surviving in a harsh land. At first they stole from the farmer Indians. Naturally they fought when they met resistance, but they didn't go out of their way to be cruel. Only later, when they met the Spaniards, did they earn the name "Tigers of the Human Species."

During the later 1500s, the Spaniards raided northward from Mexico for slaves to work their mines and ranches. The Apaches hated these bearded knights in steel armor, for they were merciless to their victims. Anyone who resisted was tortured, or crippled, or killed on the spot. Their hatred was transferred to the Mexicans, who continued slave raiding after winning their independence.

Apaches were not the sort of people to allow others to take advantage of them. It was almost as though the blazing sun had baked an adobe-hardness into them, turning them into history's most dreaded guerrilla fighters. Unlike the plains tribes, they never treated war as a game in which braves gained honor. Apaches cared nothing for the gorgeous war bonnet of the plains warriors. They never counted coup and seldom scalped their enemies; they feared the ghosts of the dead and even when they took a few scalps, they threw them away after the victory dance.

Enemies called them sneaks and cowards who'd never fight an equal number of men on equal terms. This is untrue. They were cautious, not cowardly. A practical people, they saw no reason to endanger themselves by giving enemies an even chance. Apaches fought by their own rules, nobody else's. They fought when they pleased, where, and only if the odds were heavily in their favor. Anything that saved Apache lives was all right with them no matter what others said.

Saving lives meant avoiding mass charges in the open; they never fought a Little Bighorn-style battle. The Apaches favored ambushes and lightning-quick raids by small war parties. They were also escape artists. If anything went wrong, they scattered like a flock of geese, each going in a different direction. Hours later, or even days later, when it was safe, they came together again at a pre-arranged place miles away from the attack site.

Training for the warpath began early. No Green Beret or British Commando ever went through a tougher course. Youngsters learned to depend on their own strength rather than on a horse's. By the time they reached their early teens they could run thirty miles a day, barefooted, up and down mountains and across deserts. Teams of runners could wear down a horse and rider with their steady, never-ending pace. Although good horsemen, the Apache didn't love their horses like the plains tribes. Horses were ridden to death, eaten, and fresh mounts stolen whenever necessary.

Apaches knew their home territory for hundreds of miles around. Hiding places, ambush spots, escape trails, water holes: all were familiar to the youngster before he reached his teens. Water holes were especially important in desert warfare, where the dry heat exhausts even the strongest person. When water was scarce, war parties cut the spines off the round barrel cactus and squeezed moisture from its pulp. When they found water, a horse might be killed and twenty feet of intestine removed. The slippery whitish tubing was cleaned (sort of), filled with water, and tied around a horse like a huge canteen.

The Apaches used torture to strike terror into enemies, thereby weakening their courage and will to fight. No adult white man ever lived to tell of his experiences as an Apache captive. A prisoner might be hung head down over a slow fire and roasted alive, or staked out over an anthill and smeared with wild honey, or tied to a saguaro cactus with wet rawhide and left to die as the cords dried in the sun, forcing the nail-like thorns through his body. Captured women and children were usually adopted into a band as equals.

Apache war parties stabbed deep into Mexico during the early 1800s. Not satisfied to attack the nearby states of Sonora and Chihuaha (Chi-wa-wa), they went as far as the Gulf of California. The cry "Apache! Apache!" sent people fleeing in panic to the nearest *presidio*, or fort. Raids became so bad that over a hundred settlements were abandoned for lack of soldiers to defend them.

It seemed impossible to control these marauders until the governments of Sonora and Chihuaha thought of a plan called the "Project of War." The key to the plan was the bounty it offered for Apache scalps: one hundred gold pesos for a warrior's scalp, fifty for a woman's, and twenty-five for a child's.

Scalp-taking became a business that attracted professional killers from Mexico and the United States. These men cared nothing about innocence or guilt. Business was business, to them. When they saw Apaches, they didn't see people but packets of gold coins to be gambled away or spent on whiskey in saloons on both sides of the border.

James Johnson was such a man. Johnson ran a trading post in the copper mining town of Santa Rita, New Mexico. The Mimbres Apaches thought they knew him well, and Juan José Compa, their chief, trusted him as a friend. He shouldn't have.

One day in 1837, Johnson invited the Mimbres to a *fiesta* with music, dancing, and plenty to eat. The Indians were enjoying themselves as Johnson's men placed sacks of corn on the ground and invited them to help themselves. The people crowded around, laughing as they divided the yellow kernels among themselves. What they didn't know was that Johnson had hidden a small cannon nearby, behind some brush. The cannon was loaded with bullets, nails, chains, stones, and broken bottles. Johnson lit a cigar, smiled, and stepped behind the brush.

A deafening roar was followed by screams. The giant shotgun mowed down the Mimbres as Johnson's men moved in to finish their dirty work by hand. Four hundred Indians died and were scalped in a few minutes, including Juan José Compa, whom Johnson personally shot in the back. Only a few dazed survivors managed to stagger to safety in the confusion.

Among the survivors was Mangas Coloradas, or "Red Sleeves," Juan José's relative and the Mimbres' new chief. Born about 1790, Mangas must have been a sight to see. Everything about him was oversized. His head was huge, his eyes black and deep-set, his nose hooked like a vulture's beak. He stood six feet, seven inches tall and had the strength of two ordinary men half his age. To his own people he was a gentle giant, tender and softspoken. His enemies trembled at the mention of his name.

Cruelty bred more cruelty as Mangas set out to avenge the massacre. Supply wagons from Mexico were attacked, isolating Santa Rita from the outside world. Work at the mines stopped. Stores shut down. At last the townspeople decided that it was better to try to cross the desert than starve where they were.

The summer sun beat down like the flames from a blast furnace. Scouts watched the procession out of the town from afar, but Mangas held back. He had plenty of time and wanted the heat and thirst to weaken the Santa Ritans first.

The Apaches struck on the third day, killing nearly all the townspeople. Only a few escaped, because the chief wanted them to tell their Mexican friends what to expect if they came north. The murderous James Johnson also escaped—and disappeared, as he deserved, from history.

Mangas fought for nine years to drive out the Mexicans. He didn't fight alone, for in 1846 the United States declared war on Mexico. American troops streamed down the Santa Fe Trail, bound for California and Mexico.

The Apaches welcomed these *Pinda-Lick-O-Yi* (Pinda-LICK-O-Yee), these "White-Eyes," as allies. Mangas told Army officers that his people would help them in any way. "These Mexicans are rascals," he said; "we hate and will kill them all." True, James Johnson was American, but it was wrong to blame a whole people for the crimes of a few. There were bad Apaches, too. Apaches and Americans were friends, cooperating against a common enemy.

That friendship began to sour after the Mexican War. The peace treaty that followed gave the territories of Arizona and New Mexico to the United States, and with them the Apaches. The Mexicans believed they had gotten the best of the deal, for *Los Gringos*, the Yankees, would have to worry about the Apaches from now on.

In return for these territories, the Americans promised to stop Apache raids into Mexico. Forts began to spring up near the border and other key points. The Apaches were stunned and felt betrayed. They had always gone where they pleased. And it pleased them to go to Mexico. They couldn't understand why, after so many years, they had to stop. Mexicans didn't stop being enemies just because Americans scrawled words on paper.

Mangas had hoped that the Americans would leave the Southwest after the war. But instead of leaving, settlers, especially miners, began to pour into the territory. These miners were a rough-and-ready lot. One day in 1860, some miners at Pinos Altos (Tall Pines) decided to have some "fun" with Mangas. Twelve men grabbed him from behind and tied him to a wagon wheel. A big man with bulging muscles picked up a bullwhip. Another tore the shirt off his back.

Everyone was laughing, except the chief. "Do not whip Indian," he said in a low, menacing voice. "Indian never forget."

Mangas neither winced nor cried out as the whip cut into his back; Apaches knew how to bear pain without a sign. The miners were still laughing when they cut the ropes and chased him from camp.

Whipping an innocent man was cruel—and stupid. For Mangas's pride was hurt far worse than his back. He never forgot, or forgave, the insult. From that moment on he became the enemy of all White-Eyes. The war that began that day would last on and off for twenty-five years, long after Mangas's own death. It would cost the United States thousands of lives and over fifty million dollars.

Mangas invited other Apaches to join him on the warpath. War parties came, but not the one he most hoped to see. Chief Cochise of the Chiricahuas, his son-in-law, held back. Cochise's people controlled Apache Pass through the Chiricahua Mountains of southern Arizona, an important link between the eastern and western United States. The Butterfield Overland Mail ran stagecoaches through the pass and on to California as far as San Francisco.

Courage and wisdom combined in Cochise to make an unusual person: a warrior who loved peace. Cochise hoped that Indians and whites would learn to live together. When the Butterfield company asked permission to build a stagecoach depot at the head of Apache Pass, he gladly agreed. He even moved his village close by so that the Chiricahuas could

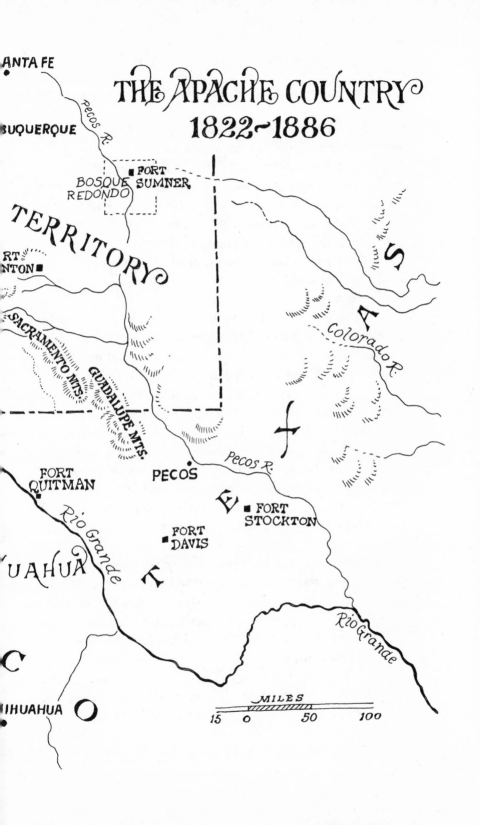

THE APACHE COUNTRY 1822~1886

ANTA FE

BUQUERQUE

Pecos R.

FORT SUMNER

BOSQUE REDONDO

TERRITORY

RT NTON

SACRAMENTO MTS.

GUADALUPE MTS.

A S

Colorado R.

FORT QUITMAN

PECOS

Pecos R.

E

FORT STOCKTON

FORT DAVIS

Rio Grande

UAHUA

T

Rio Grande

C

IHUAHUA

MILES

15 0 50 100

exchange hay and firewood for blankets and other useful things.

The peace was suddenly shattered in February, 1861, when Apaches of another band took cattle and kidnapped a boy from a ranch in the area. The ranch owner rode to Fort Buchanan, whose commander sent a cavalry detachment to track down the thieves. Lieutenant George N. Bascom, the detachment's commander, was the worst person for the job. A recent graduate of West Point, he thought he knew everything there was to know about Indians. A redskin was a redskin, and none could be trusted, according to Bascom. Threats and force were all they understood.

The lieutenant had many lessons to learn. Somehow he got the idea into his head that Cochise was behind the raid. Nothing could change his mind, including his own men, who knew the Chiricahuas and insisted they were friendly.

As soon as he made camp in Apache Pass, Bascom sent word that he wanted to see Cochise. The chief, who liked to be sociable, came along with several friends and relatives.

The moment they entered Bascom's tent he demanded the return of the boy and the cattle. At first Cochise smiled, thinking the officer was playing a practical joke. The smile turned to a scowl when he saw soldiers take positions around the tent with fixed bayonets. Bascom had lured them into a trap.

Bascom repeated his demand. Cochise replied that he knew nothing about the raid, but could find out and let him know in a day or so. "Liar!" and Bascom, shouting into the chief's face. The word stung like a whiplash. Cochise was an honorable man; indeed, Apaches were taught from childhood that lying was sinful.

A war whoop burst from Cochise's lips. A knife flashed in his hand. Before the soldiers realized what was happening, the chief had slashed open the tent wall and was running for the hills. His six companions weren't so quick. A bayonet pinned one to the ground, while the others were held hostage at gunpoint.

Cochise also knew how to take hostages. Within two hours his braves waylaid a stagecoach in the pass and took six prisoners. Bascom and Cochise were even-up: six to six.

An Apache war party rode within calling distance of the soldiers' camp. Six horsemen held lariats, each tied round the neck of a trembling white man. Cochise called across, saying that he only wanted an even exchange, nothing more, nothing less. Bascom refused. He wanted that boy and those cattle returned *pronto,* immediately. There was nothing else to discuss.

Reinforcements arrived next day and Boscom started back to the fort. In the distance the soldiers noticed buzzards circling near the trail. A horrible sight met them as they drew near. Cochise had given up on Bascom. This man was a *tonto,* a fool, and there was no reasoning with him. If Bascom wouldn't return his people, then he'd have his revenge. The hostages were tortured to death Apache style. Bascom immediately had his Indian hostages hung on the spot in reprisal. At last Mangas had his best ally.

Cochise swore to punish the White-Eyes many times over. For every Apache killed, he'd kill ten of them. And he kept his word. Small wagon trains just disappeared. Stagecoaches didn't dare venture into Apache Pass. He drove the settlers out of Tubac and burned it; it is a ghost town today. He boldly cut off Tucson, Arizona's main town, for days at a time. His braves shot settlers and ran off their cattle within sight of the town's walls. The *Arizonian* newspaper reported that, "within six months nine-tenths of the whole male population have been killed off, and every ranch, farm and mine in the country has been abandoned in consequence."

But help was on the way. Early in July, 1862, Cochise's

lookouts noticed a dust cloud rising over the western desert. Using some low hills as a screen, they approached for a closer look. What they saw startled them, for two thousand soldiers were on the march. Brigadier General James H. Carleton's California Volunteers were moving east to fight the Apaches and join the Union forces in the Civil War.

After marching forty miles across the desert, the soldiers were hot, tired, and out of water. Another day without water would mean the end of most of them. And the only water in the area was the cool, bubbling spring at the top of Apache Pass. Here's where the Indians would have to fight their battle.

Cochise sent word for Mangas to join him, and together they had a force of seven hundred braves. The chiefs planned carefully. Boulders were rolled into place to form a waist-high barricade. Sniper holes were dug into the cliffside.

The Californians arrived on schedule. Toward afternoon, July 15, an advance guard of one hundred fifty men under Captain Thomas Roberts halted at the entrance to the pass. It was quiet, too quiet.

The hidden Apaches watched as two cavalrymen slowly rode forward, their eyes scanning the towering cliffs. Minutes passed. The scouts turned and motioned their comrades to come ahead.

Cavalry and infantry advanced, followed by a line of mule-drawn wagons. Behind the main body, still out of sight, two cannon bumped and lurched over the uneven ground.

Hi-Yi-i-i-i . . . Hi-Yi-i-i-i. The shrill war cry rang out, echoing down the valley. Showers of bullets and arrows sent the soldiers running out of the pass as fast as they could go. Yet there was no safety outside, for they had to have water soon.

Captain Roberts regrouped his troops and sent them back into the pass, this time in battle formation. The thirsty men fought fiercely, inching forward until only a few hundred

yards from the lifegiving spring. The Apaches held their
ground, determined to keep the water.

They were doing well until a high-pitched scream
sounded overhead, followed by an explosion and a shower
of rock splinters. At last Roberts's cannon had joined the
action. Shells slammed into the cliffsides, searching out the
hidden Apaches and smashing their defenses. It was the
soldiers' turn to cheer now. With a shout of victory, they
charged up to the spring. As some blazed away at the enemy,
others lay on their bellies, sucking up the water and pouring
it on their heads. The sun set and Apache Pass was still.
Sixty-five braves had died, mostly because of exploding shells,
compared to three soldiers.

The battle, though, was not over. Cochise and Mangas
retreated up the pass and prepared another defense line.
Roberts, too, knew that plenty of fighting still lay ahead. As
soon as the sun peaked over the eastern hills, he sent messengers back to the main column for reinforcements.

Apache lookouts saw the messengers leave and told their
chiefs. Immediately Mangas and fifty braves sprang into the
saddle to head them off.

The soldiers rode for their lives, firing over their shoulders
as they rode at breakneck speed. One soldier fell, then another,
rolling over and over in the choking dust until they lay still.
The Apaches were gaining.

Private John Teal's horse began to lag behind. The animal
was exhausted and no whip or spurs could make it run faster.
A bullet stopped its running forever.

Although stunned by the fall, Private Teal managed to
crawl behind the carcass. He was in the open. Escape was impossible. His only hope was to shoot as many Indians as possible and go down fighting.

The soldier picked out the biggest Indian, aimed, and
pulled the trigger of his rifle. The warrior tumbled from the

saddle, a bullet in his chest. The other braves instantly reined in their horses, forgetting about Teal. The battle of Apache Pass was over, ended by a single bullet.

Private Teal had shot Mangas Coloradas. The chief was still alive, but would die without medical attention. Braves placed him on his horse and headed for the nearest doctor, who was a hundred miles away in Janos, Mexico. One brave led Mangas's horse, while another sat behind him, holding him upright in his arms.

Janos knew it was in trouble when scores of grim Apache warriors suddenly took over the streets. Without knocking, nine warriors carried their chief into the doctor's house. "Listen well," said one in broken Spanish, "you make Indian well. If he lives, everybody lives. If he dies, everybody dies— you first."

As his wife and children looked on, the doctor began the treatment carefully. *Very carefully.* He worked on the unconscious Indian all night by candlelight. By dawn, he had the bullet out and the wound bandaged. Mangas would live. So would Janos. *"Gracias a Dios,"* thanks be to God, the doctor sighed.

In the meantime, General Carleton moved against the Chiricahua and their allies. A fort—Fort Bowie—was built to command the approaches to Apache Pass. The pass became so dangerous that Cochise had to move to the Dragoon Mountains further west.

General Carleton kept up the pressure during the months that followed. He gave orders, in writing, that all Apache men "are to be slain whenever and wherever they can be found," even if they seemed peaceful. Apache women and children were to be captured and kept in camps under armed guard. Although this cruel order was usually not carried out, the Indians suffered greatly. Within a year one of Carleton's officers had rounded up the Mescalero Apaches and Navajos

Colonel Kit Carson, a veteran Indian fighter, was the colonel who sent the Mescalero Apaches and Navajos to Bosque Redondo Reservation.

and sent them to the Bosque Redondo (Round Grove), a reservation on the Pecos River. The officer's name was Colonel Kit Carson.

Mangas Coloradas never saw a reservation. After recovering from his wound, he returned to his people. The old man had lost weight, but was as strong as ever. Yet he had changed, inside. He had done a lot of thinking in Mexico and come to realize that the White-Eyes were in the Southwest to stay. No matter how many he killed, others would take their places. If a chance for peace came, he'd take it.

One day a message arrived at the Mimbres' camp under a flag of truce. Mangas was invited to come to an Army camp near Pinos Altos to discuss peace. He must come alone and unarmed, but he'd be safe under Army protection. "Don't go," said his warriors, suspecting a trick.

Soldiers arrested the chief the moment he set foot in their camp. That night, January 17, 1863, Colonel J.R. West spoke to his two guards. "Men, that old murderer has left a trail of blood five hundred miles long. I want him dead or alive to-morrow morning. Do you understand? *I want him dead."*

They understood. As Mangas slept, a guard held the point of his bayonet in the campfire until it became red hot, then jabbed it into the chief's leg. As soon as Mangas leaped up, startled and crying out in pain, both guards opened fire. The official report said he died while trying to escape.

Cochise continued the war, more determined than ever to punish the treacherous White-Eyes. Nothing the army did seemed to work against him. The Dragoon Mountains were a natural fortress. The Chiricahuas left their hideouts by secret trails, attacked, and returned by other secret trails. If soldiers chased them, they scattered. Or they sprang an ambush. Warriors lay motionless, their bronze-colored bodies blending with the desert sands, until a patrol passed, then opened fire from behind. No Army command dared follow them into the unmapped maze of mountains that loomed in the distance.

In September, 1872, two high-ranking Army officers arrived in Apache country, one to make peace, the other to make war if he failed. The peacemaker was Oliver Otis Howard,

"The Praying General." Howard knew that Cochise would never come to him, not after what happened to Mangas. If he wanted a meeting, he'd have to go to the Dragoon Mountain alone or with a small cavalry escort.

In ten years only one soldier had gone into the Dragoons and come out alive. Captain Thomas Jeffords, or Taglito (Red Beard), was the only white man Cochise trusted. He had once managed a mail-carrying service between Fort Bowie and Tucson. The Apaches killed so many of his drivers that he decided to settle matters with Cochise man to man.

Taking his life in his hands, Jeffords found his way to the Chiricahua camp. Cochise was a brave man who admired bravery in others, and the sight of this red-bearded man coming into his camp alone drew his admiration. He invited Jeffords to sit cross-legged on his blanket and talk things over. The more they spoke, the more they liked each other. Jeffords visited Cochise many times after that. Their friendship deepened until one day they cut their wrists slightly and pressed the open wounds together. Indian and white man's blood mingled, making them blood brothers.

Jeffords was General Howard's passport into the Dragoons. The two men rode onward until they met a group of Apache warriors. Leading them was a six-footer, broad-shouldered, with long black hair and large, dark eyes; his face was painted a bright scarlet red. *"Buenos días, señor,"* said Cochise.

The chief asked why Howard had come on so dangerous a journey. The general explained that he came in peace to make peace. "No one wants peace more than I," Cochise replied. "The Apaches made peace before, and it was not the Apache that broke the peace." Howard could only nod his head in agreement and say that he wanted the new peace to last forever. Cochise smiled and promised to begin the peace council in a few days, when his leading warriors arrived.

177

The days of waiting were an education for the general. For the first time he saw Indians not as fearsome savages, but as human beings. The children were shy, but soft words and sweet biscuits soon had them snuggling against him. He taught Cochise's son, Natchez, to write his name. The children taught him Apache words and giggled when he mispronounced them.

On the third day lookouts reported soldiers in the distance. The whole camp ran to Howard, and everyone was frightened. For a moment the veteran campaigner felt their fear, knew what it meant to be hunted. It was a false alarm, only soldiers bringing messages from Fort Bowie.

Another day Howard noticed a fancy rifle that had belonged to an officer killed by Apaches. As he stared at the gun, Cochise, who had been watching his face, said softly: "No triste, General!" "Don't be sad, general." Cochise knew what was in his mind and added in Spanish, "You know, General, that we do things in war that we do not do in peace." Howard looked up, his eyes watery, and said that he had been in war for many years. He prayed for a time when there would be no more war.

Good will made the peace talks go smoothly. Rather than force the Chiricahuas to a faraway reservation, Howard agreed that their reservation should be their homeland: the Chiricahua and Dragoon Mountains and everything in between. Cochise was happy. "Hereafter," he said, "the white man and the Indian are to drink the same water, eat the same bread, and be at peace." He meant it.

As Howard prepared to leave, Cochise put his arms around him. "Good-bye," he said in perfect English. The Chiricahuas loved this one-armed soldier who spoke truth and treated them as equals. From Arizona he went to California, then up the coast to Oregon, to the land of the Nez Percé.

Although Cochise made peace, other bands remained on

General George Crook commanded the army in the Southwest.
Although he fought the Indians, he felt that they were often in the
right and driven to war by dishonest whites.

the warpath. These bands became the responsibility of Howard's assistant, Lieutenant Colonel George Crook.

Crook was one of the finest soldiers ever to serve his country. He stood six feet tall in his stockings, was ramrod straight, and strong as a bull. A bristling beard covered his face. The beard parted naturally at the chin, and he sometimes tied the ends with colorful ribbons. Uniforms made him uncomfortable. His favorite outfit was a hunting suit of lightweight canvas and a sun helmet.

Indians called Crook "The Gray Fox," because he was so clever and sly. Whenever he had some free time, he went hunting. Often he went away four days with no companion but his mule, named Apache, and his dog. Once Crook found a trail he stuck to it no matter where it led or how dangerous his prey. A crack shot, he could bring down a seven-hundred-pound grizzly bear with a single bullet.

Crook, like Howard, respected the Indian as a human being. He believed that greedy and stupid whites, including soldiers, were more to blame for the troubles in the West than the tribes. Although he always spoke in a low voice, his words carried the sting of truth. "The American Indian," he told a graduating class at West Point, "commands respect for his rights only so long as he inspires terror for his rifle."

Respect for Indian rights didn't mean that Crook was soft. Far from it. Howard had made a good peace, and Crook didn't intend to see it wrecked by anyone. The holdouts would have to put down their weapons or be destroyed.

Other commanders had fought the Apaches "by the book." Large bodies of well-equipped troops moved slowly, hoping to avoid ambushes and crush the enemy by weight of numbers. They failed. The Apaches outwitted them because they were physically tough and able to get along with only the barest necessities. Fair enough. Crook would fight the Apaches by turning his troopers into white—and black—Apaches.

Crook hardened his troopers by sending them on seventy-mile "stripped saddle" marches across the desert in summer. It was so hot, men said, that you'd have to tie two thermometers together to tell the temperature. Only basic supplies were taken along. Soldiers didn't wash, because soap took up space and water was precious. They learned to shave with pieces of glass from broken bottles. And they lost weight from loss of body water. Sometimes, when water ran out and they thought they'd die of thirst, they opened their horses' veins to moisten their lips with blood. A few died of thirst or sunstroke, but the survivors became first-class desert fighters.

Crook's army nickname was "The Granddaddy of the Pack Mules." It was a name he deserved, for instead of having supplies hauled by wagon, he used mules. These animals were ideal for long treks in rugged country. Strong and sure-footed, they could go round the clock without water. Crook redesigned the mule pack to allow an animal to carry three hundred twenty-five pounds instead of the usual one hundred twenty-five pounds and finish a march in good condition. Crook's methods were still being used by the United States Army during the Korean War of the 1950s.

The rule of guerrilla warfare is to find the enemy's trail and stay with it until he is cornered and forced to surrender or be wiped out. To find the trail, Crook hired Apache scouts, who knew every inch of the countryside. Apache bands often had grudges against each other and men gladly enlisted for revenge and a soldier's pay; thirteen dollars a month seemed like a lot of money a hundred years ago. Crook never could have defeated the Apaches without the help of their own people.

Crook's orders were simple: once a trail was discovered, it must be followed even if supplies ran out and the chase lasted for weeks. The troopers could live like Apaches, filling in rations with whatever they could find on the desert, including barbecued sidewinder rattlesnake. Yet hard living didn't dampen their spirits. One officer remembered how his men would gather around the campfire pounding on tin cans and singing Indian war songs with deep Irish accents.

Speed, endurance, and fighting spirit proved a winning

combination. The cavalry wore down Apache resistance in dozens of small fights in out-of-the-way places. By summer, 1874, the Apaches of Arizona and New Mexico had given up and moved to reservations.

Crook's job, however, was far from being finished. He was not a jailer who locked up his prisoners and threw away the key. For peace to last, he knew that the Apaches had to be able to support themselves without raiding. Firmly, patiently, he encouraged them to learn farming and stock raising. He also dug irrigation canals, built roads, and strung hundreds of miles of telegraph lines. Slowly the Apaches got used to the way of life he mapped out for thim. The War Department in Washington was so happy with his success that it promoted him to brigadier general and sent him north—to face the Sioux.

The Southwest enjoyed peace for the next few years. Even after Cochise died in 1874, the Apaches stayed on their reservations. Yet they grew restless. Things weren't working out as they'd hoped. Part of the trouble was their own fault. Younger men became bored with farm chores and missed the excitement of the warpath. Peace began to pinch like a tight boot.

Even so, most Apaches would have been satisfied with reservation life had they felt they were being treated fairly. But as soon as Crook left, the "Tucson Ring" began playing its dirty games. The Tucson Ring was a gang of dishonest politicians and traders who'd do anything to fill their pockets. Wagon loads of government supplies meant for the Indians were sold to mining camps. Scales were rigged to give false weights and official records forged to cover up the thievery.

Things really became dangerous in 1877, when the government tried to save money by moving the Apache bands to one large reservation. San Carlos in eastern Arizona was chosen because the land seemed worthless. The soldiers stationed at nearby Fort Apache hated the place, calling it "Hell's Forty Acres." Bone-dry and whipped by fiery winds, nothing but sagebrush and scrawny cottonwoods grew there. When a little rain did fall, flies and gnats swarmed in the millions.

The Tucson Ring swept away all of Howard's and Crook's good work. Once again the Indians saw that treaties made to last forever lasted only as long as no money was to be made by breaking them. The Apaches were not asked to give up their old reservations. They were told to pack up and get out—or else. Rather than starve slowly at San Carlos, hundreds broke away.

Most reservation-jumpers returned to their familiar haunts in the mountains. Others, however, found their safest hideouts not in the United States, but in the mountains of Mexico. Traveling by night, a handful of warriors could slip across the border anywhere along the thousand miles from Arizona to Texas. They struck swiftly, ruthlessly, leaving a trail of dead ranchers and burned ranches wherever they passed.

Five thousand soldiers—one third of the fighting strength of the United States Army—were unable to stop the raiders. Soldiers couldn't be everywhere, guarding the border *and* protecting settlements at the same time. Nor was it enough to find a trail and stick to it. Often a cavalry patrol nearly caught up with a war party, only to give up the chase at the border. The Apaches, safely across, waved and fired their rifles in the air, while the cavalrymen shouted curses and turned back.

Here was a job for General George Crook. As soon as he returned to the Southwest in September, 1882, he began to win back the Apaches' confidence. Risking his life, he rode into the mountains with a small cavalry escort to visit the runaways' camps and listen to their grievances. The Apache had no love for the whiskered general, but they respected him and trusted him to keep his word. Within a few weeks, he persuaded most of the bands to return to San Carlos.

Living conditions began to improve. Crook had dishonest Indian agents thrown off the reservation and replaced by loyal army officers. Food supplies arrived regularly. By year's end only a few tiny bands remained at large in Mexico.

Yet the worst was still to come. For although the United States and Mexican governments agreed that soldiers of each nation could cross the border after Apaches, these border bands were the toughest of all.

A group of Apache scouts formed by General Crook to help him track down and fight reservation-jumpers.

184

Their leader was a dark-faced, muscular man five feet eight inches tall and weighing one hundred seventy pounds. His eyes shone like bits of black glass with a fire burning behind them. His mouth was straight, thin-lipped, and strong. Old bullet holes, some large enough to hold small pebbles, dotted his body. "Bullets cannot kill me!" he'd shout. Enemies called him "the worst Indian who ever lived." His name was Geronimo.

He hadn't always been a fierce warrior. Born into the tribe of Mangas Coloradas about 1829, his childhood name was Goyathlay. The name means "He Who Yawns," for he was probably easygoing and a little lazy. The name Geronimo (Jerome) was given to him by the Mexicans who used Christian names to identify especially bold Indians.

At the age of seventeen, Geronimo married his childhood sweetheart, a lovely girl named Alope. The couple had three children and, together with his widowed mother, lived happily.

Their happiness might have continued had it not been for the Mexicans. In 1858, the Mimbres Apaches were at peace with the government of Chihuaha. Mangas led his band south on a trading visit to Janos. It was to be a vacation and everyone looked forward to having a good time.

Disaster followed. While the warriors were busily trading in town, soldiers surrounded the camp. No guards were posted, and the camp was filled with women, children, and old people. General Carasco ordered his men not to use their guns, since shooting would bring the warriors rushing back. The soldiers attacked with swords, bayonets and axes, killing and scalping the helpless Indians. A few were spared, to be sold into slavery.

The Mimbres warriors returned to find their camp a shambles. For a moment they stood in shocked silence, then began searching frantically for their families.

Geronimo's family lay close together, dead. The young

brave nearly went crazy with grief. That night the warriors held a council to decide what to do. Geronimo sat silently while the others voted to return to Arizona. They were surrounded by Mexicans, and there was no hope of fighting successfully. Years later Geronimo recalled: "Our chief gave the order to start at once in perfect silence for our homes in Arizona, leaving the dead where they lay upon the field. I stood until all had passed, hardly knowing what I would do. I had no weapon, nor did I hardly wish to fight, neither did I think of recovering the bodies of my loved ones, for that was forbidden. I had no purpose left. I finally followed the tribe silently, keeping just within hearing distance of the soft noise of the feet."

Never again was Geronimo easygoing or lazy. Hatred filled him, until his whole life became a routine of fighting and preparing to fight. Mangas recognized his abilities and made him leader of the avenging war parties. At least twice a year he raided Mexico, killing, torturing, and burning as he went. Mangas's war with the Americans merely gave Geronimo's hatred another target. And when Mangas died, he joined Cochise's Chiricahuaha, adopting them as his people and making their war his own.

Geronimo was the only leader who refused to accept Cochise's peace treaty with General Howard. He spoke in the council, demanding to know what right the Americans had to move the Apaches off land that had been theirs since time began. "Let those come with me who would dare help drive them out, so that Apache lands will belong to Apache people!" he cried.

A few braves joined him with their families; Geronimo had remarried and was raising another family. They were completely on their own, outlaws even from their own people. Campsites were chosen high in the Sierra Madres, the Mexican section of the Rocky Mountains chain. Steep and rugged,

Geronimo was the most dreaded of all Apacht warriors. He especially liked to fight Mexicans, who had massacred his whole family.

Although old and nearly crippled, Nana outwitted every Army detachment sent after him. He later joined Geronimo in the Sierra Madre Mountains of Mexico.

cut by deep canyons, the towering Sierra Madres have some of the roughest terrain in the New World.

At the very moment General Crook was visiting the runaways from San Carlos, Geronimo returned and persuaded three hundred people to come to the Sierra Madres. Bands led by Cochise's son, Natchez, and Mangas, son of Mangas Coloradas, joined him. There were also lesser chiefs like Chato, Loco, Bonito, and Chihuaha.

You'd never know it by looking at him, but one of Geronimo's ablest men was a Mimbres Apache in his late seventies. Nana, although wrinkled, half blind, and partially crippled with rheumatism, was a master of desert warfare. With only forty men, he once led a thousand troops on a wild goose chase across a thousand miles of desert. They never caught him; indeed, he caught them in ambushes several times. Nana fought eight battles, winning them all without losing a man.

Geronimo's raiders ran circles around the cavalry, making the settlers desperate. "Where's the army?" "Why isn't it protecting us?" they demanded to know. Washington heard their complaints and sent General Crook a telegram: "GO WHERE YOU MUST BUT GET GERONIMO DEAD OR ALIVE."

Into Mexico after Geronimo. General Crook with his favorite riding mule, Apache, and two Apache scouts.

Crook meant to get Geronimo alive, if possible. Enough blood had already been shed and nothing good could come from shedding more. Instead of driving into Mexico with a whole army, he came with two hundred fifty cavalry and Apache scouts. Their mission was to talk Geronimo out of the mountains without a fight.

Crook's force crossed the scorching desert and began to climb the Sierra Madres. The going became so rough that pack mules lost their footing and fell hundreds of feet to the canyons below. Weeks passed without seeing an Apache, although they knew Apache eyes were on them always. Geronimo had lookouts on mountaintops with captured field glasses; messages were flashed for hundreds of miles, from mountaintop to mountaintop, with mirrors.

At last the scouts surprised some women from Chihuaha's band. They were tired of running and spending sleepless nights filled with fear. One of them agreed to carry Crook's peace offer to Geronimo's camp.

The leaders met on May 23, 1883. Geronimo said he was willing to surrender if Crook promised to treat his people fairly at San Carlos. The general nodded his head in agreement. But there was more. Geronimo said he needed extra time to round up his scattered people. If Crook went ahead, he'd come into United States territory later.

Again Crook nodded in agreement. Geronimo, he knew, really wanted to surrender, otherwise he wouldn't have come to the meeting to begin with. Next day, Crook started back with three hundred twenty-five Apaches, including most of the war chiefs. Only Geronimo and Chato stayed behind until later.

How long is "later"? Days melted into months without sign of Geronimo. The Tuscon Ring was overjoyed, since it finally had something to hold against Crook. It paid newspapers to print articles saying that the general had been

Geronimo and Nachez, son of Cochise, ride out to meet General Crook. Standing at the left is Geronimo's own son, Chapo.

tricked and demanding his replacement. Just when things looked darkest, Geronimo crossed the border, February, 1884, with the rest of his people. He had kept his word. The only disagreement was over the herd of stolen cattle he brought along. Crook had the cattle taken away and sold at auction, the money going to pay the owners.

Geronimo soon grew tired of reservation life. True, he could go anywhere on San Carlos. His family had food to eat and could sleep through the night unafraid. Yet something was missing. He wasn't free.

On the night of May 17, 1885, Geronimo, Mangas, Chihuaha, and Nana got drunk and decided to return to the Sierra Madres. When they asked Chato to come along, he refused. Chato was sober and knew that running away would make things harder for those left behind. Forty-two men and boys, plus ninety-two women and children, took to the hills, cutting the telegraph wires as they went.

THE APACHES HAVE BROKEN OUT! screamed the newspaper headlines. Troops were called up on both sides of the border to deal with them once and for all. The Mexican army put thousands of men into the field, as if a major war had begun. In addition, the government released hundreds of convicts from prison and formed them into military units called Irregulars. The Irregulars were merely *banditos* in uniform. They did their best to avoid Apaches, saving their ammunition and their courage for robbing their fellow Mexicans.

The manhunt went nonstop for ten months. Geronimo's band did not flee like frightened jackrabbits. It fought, dodged, defended itself, attacked, and escaped time after time. Food and horses were never a problem, for Mexican *ranchos* were easy to capture.

Still, everyone knew the chase couldn't last forever. Luckily for Geronimo, Crook's scouts located his band before the Mexicans, otherwise everyone would have been massacred.

On March 26, 1886, the general and the chief faced each other again at the Cañon de los Embudos—The Canyon of Funnels—ten miles south of the border. Crook was stern as he looked his enemy in the eyes. "You must make up your minds whether you will stay out on the warpath or surrender unconditionally. If you stay out I'll keep after you and kill the last one if it takes fifty years."

After much discussion, Geronimo and his braves made their decision. "Two or three words are enough," Geronimo told Crook. "I surrender to you. We are all comrades, all one family. What others say I say also. I give myself up to you. Do with me as you please. I surrender. Once I moved about like the wind. Now I surrender to you, and that is all." The two men shook hands to seal their bargain.

Crook set out for Fort Bowie after leaving behind some soldiers to bring back the Indians next day. Meanwhile, Bob Tribollet, a wandering whiskey seller for the Tucson Ring, found Geronimo's camp. The Apaches were downhearted, and Tribollet easily filled them with alcohol and lies about how they'd be hung the moment they set foot in Arizona. Geronimo and thirty-eight Apaches, including eighteen warriors, fled to the mountains once again. The War Department accused General Crook of being too lenient with Indians and removed him as commander in the southwest.

Crook's replacement was Nathan A. Miles, promoted to brigadier general for his role in the Nez Percé war. Miles wasn't taking any chances this time. Five thousand American soldiers and five hundred Apache scouts joined thousands of Mexican troops in the manhunt. In Arizona and New Mexico, thousands of cowboys and settlers patrolled the countryside. Every water hole was guarded, every ranchhouse defended like a small fort. The Signal Corps set up heliostats, large mirrors for flashing Morse code messages, on mountaintops for hundreds of miles in every direction.

Miles also formed a unit of picked desert fighters and Apache scouts to spearhead the manhunt. To command this outfit he selected Captain Henry W. Lawton. Lawton called his outfit a "flying column," because it could march a whole day without stopping and go eighteen hours without a drop of water.

Tracking Geronimo turned out to be worse than fighting him. One day Lawton's column climbed an eight-thousand-foot mountain. Next day it plunged into the valley and crossed a stretch of desert where the sun was so strong that men burned their hands if they touched the metal of their guns. Pack mules were left behind when they couldn't keep up the pace. Only men endured, and even they collapsed from heat and thirst.

Geronimo, meanwhile, drove his people without mercy. Every trick was used to throw their pursuers off the trail. Horses' hooves were wrapped in animal skins so as not to leave footprints; people often jumped from rock to rock for the same reason. Still, Lawton's Apache scouts found the trail. The hunt continued, although hunters and hunted were exhausted.

For six months the hunt continued without a result. At last Geronimo saw that his people couldn't go on against such odds. The world seemed filled with enemies to fight, but not enough places to hide. He sent word to General Miles that he wanted to discuss peace terms. Miles, in reply, sent Lieutenant Charles B. Gatewood into the Sierra Madres as his personal representative.

Lawton's flying column was only a few hours behind Geronimo when Gatewood arrived on August 24, 1886. They met in a peaceful valley. Geronimo looked tired, his hand trembling as he wiped the sweat from his forehead. He wanted to hear Miles's message.

Gatewood gave it to him straight: "Surrender, and you will be sent with your families to Florida with the other Indians. Accept these terms or fight it out."

Florida! The named seemed so strange, so distant to these desert people. "The Land of Flowers" wasn't of Geronimo's world.

Geronimo returned to his people in the hills to tell them of the general's terms. They didn't want to leave the Southwest, but it was that or a fight to the death. It was a hard choice, one they were unable to make for themselves. At last Geronimo rode into Gatewood's camp and said, "We have spoken together for many hours but still do not know what to do. We want your advice. Consider yourself not a white man but one of us. Remember all that has been said today and tell us what we should do."

Geronimo's request took Gatewood by surprise. They were enemies, but also human beings. Gatewood was being asked to decide for them not as a soldier but as a person. He sat silently for a moment, deep in thought, then said, "Trust General Miles and surrender to him."

Geronimo nodded his head in agreement. "All right, we surrender. Let us go to General Miles." And so, with those words, Apache warfare ended forever.

The war ended, but the Apaches' troubles continued for many years thereafter. President Grover Cleveland broke the

On the way to exile. Geronimo, third from right, sits with some of his warriors near the railroad train that will take them to Fort Marion, Florida. Note the armed guards near the steps and the soldier keeping an eye on them from beneath the car.

surrender agreement the moment he heard its terms. Geronimo, he believed, should be hanged, not sent to live in Florida at taxpayers' expense.

Instead of uniting the warriors with their families at Fort Marion, Florida, they were sent to Fort Pickens several hundred miles away. Not only were the reservation-jumpers sent into exile, but the scouts who had served the army so loyally were forced to go along with them. The government had decided to make a clean sweep of the Chiricahuaha and Mimbres once and for all.

The hot, damp climate of Florida took its toll. The Indians, who were used to the dry heat of the Southwest, sickened and died in scores, especially the children. Two years later, 1888, the survivors were transferred to Mount Vernon Barracks, Alabama, then to Fort Sill, Oklahoma, in 1894. When Geronimo died there in 1909, he was still a prisoner of war.

The rest of his people were held as war prisoners until 1915, when they were loaded into boxcars and shipped to the Mescalero Apache reservation in New Mexico. Finally, once again the Chiricahuas and Mimbres could taste the warm desert dust and feel the dry wind on their skin.

seven

The Ghosts of Wounded Knee

When Sitting Bull's Hunkpapa Sioux escaped to Canada in 1877 they swore never to return to the United States. There was nothing to go back to, they felt, except bad memories. Their ancient hunting grounds were barren, the game killed off. Railroad men and cattlemen, miners and farmers, were changing the face of the land. Worst of all, they distrusted the United States Government, which had made fifty-two treaties with the Sioux and kept none of them. "There is no talking to these Americans," said Sitting Bull. "They are all liars. You cannot believe anything they say."

The Hunkpapas' only hope of starting new lives was Canada, and that country made them feel unwelcome. The Canadian government gave them no help of any sort. No food. No clothing. No shelter. All they'd get from Canada was protection so long as they behaved themselves. The Canadians had their own Indians to take care of and didn't want strangers swarming across the border.

Sitting Bull's people gradually became discouraged and

Hard times. When they returned from Canada, Sitting Bull, shown here with his family, and his people had to live in tipis covered with thin canvas, instead of the usual buffalo hides.

decided to return to the United States. Singly or in family groups, they surrendered to the troops at the border. At last, in June, 1881, Sitting Bull came in with nearly two hundred followers. Even he had become a reservation Indian.

The Sioux leader was sent to Standing Rock Reservation, South Dakota, where he lived with his family in a cabin beside the Grand River. Although defeated, his people still looked up to him. Once, when a commission came from Washington to talk the Sioux into giving up part of the reservation, he spoke out against the deal. Senator Dawes, the commission's chairman, tried to stop him from speaking, but Sitting Bull was determined to have the last word. He waved his hand and, Senator or not, the Sioux rose as one man and followed him out of the meeting.

Sitting Bull was permitted to leave Standing Rock only once, in 1885. He left not as a free man, but as a circus curiosity. Buffalo Bill Cody had given up scouting for show business. He started a traveling wild west show to give the "tenderfeet" back east a taste of the frontier. And what would be better than to show them Sitting Bull, the greatest of Indian leaders?

Sitting Bull, circus performer. The great Hunkpapa leader poses with Buffalo Bill during his tour with the Wild West Show in 1885.

Buffalo Bill was right. Everywhere crowds turned out to see the "Killer of Custer." Sometimes they booed, but after the performance they lined up to buy his picture. Sitting Bull gave most of the money to the beggar boys who followed him everywhere. Such poverty puzzled the old warrior. He once told Miss Annie Oakley, the show's top sharpshooter, that he couldn't understand how whites could be so unkind to their own poor.

Sitting Bull had enough of show business after one season. He returned to the reservation with a little money and a gift from Buffalo Bill—a horse trained to sit down and raise a hoof at the sound of a gunshot. Whatever happened from now on, Sitting Bull had decided to spend his remaining years among his own people.

These were hard years for the western Indians, years in which everything they knew and loved was being swept away. Long before, in the time of the grandfathers' grandfathers, a Sioux holy man named Drinks Water had a dream. He woke up shaking, it scared him so. He dreamed that all the animals had disappeared into the earth and that strangers had woven a spider's web around the Indians. "When this happens," he said, "you shall live in square houses, in a barren land, and beside those square gray houses you shall starve." That dream was coming true.

Food on the reservations was scarce and getting scarcer, as Congress cut the rations. Indians often had to travel ninety miles for their rations, and then couldn't eat everything they received. It was against the rules to eat cow's intestines, a delicacy among the Plains tribes.

The clothing given was never enough, and tipis covered with canvas instead of buffalo hide gave little protection against the Dakota winters. Other Indians had to get used to sleeping in drafty wooden cabins.

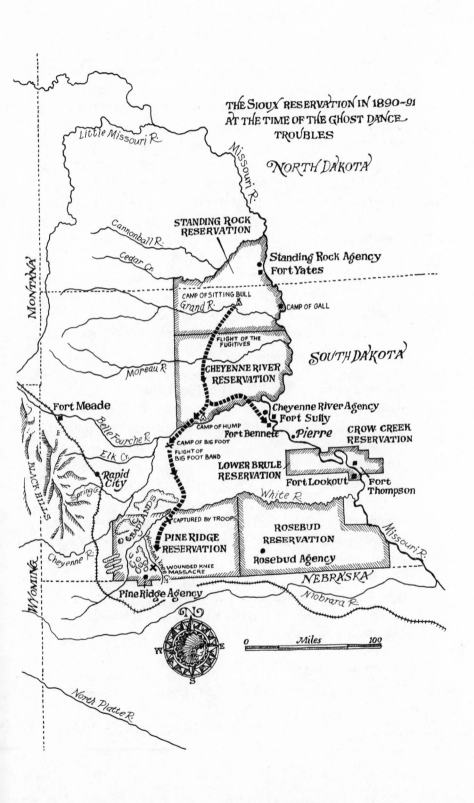

THE SIOUX RESERVATION IN 1890~91
AT THE TIME OF THE GHOST DANCE
TROUBLES

NORTH DAKOTA

Little Missouri R.

Missouri R.

MONTANA

Cannonball R.

Cedar Cr.

STANDING ROCK
RESERVATION

Standing Rock Agency
Fort Yates

CAMP OF SITTING BULL

Grand R.

CAMP OF GALL

FLIGHT OF THE
FUGITIVES

SOUTH DAKOTA

Moreau R.

CHEYENNE RIVER
RESERVATION

Fort Meade

Belle Fourche R.

Elk Cr.

CAMP OF HUMP

Cheyenne River Agency
Fort Sully

Fort Bennett

Pierre

CROW CREEK
RESERVATION

CAMP OF BIG FOOT

FLIGHT OF
BIG FOOT BAND

LOWER BRULE
RESERVATION

BLACK HILLS

Springs

Rapid
City

Fort Lookout

Fort
Thompson

White R.

BADLANDS

CAPTURED BY TROOPS

Wounded Knee Cr.

ROSEBUD
RESERVATION

Missouri R.

Cheyenne R.

PINE RIDGE
RESERVATION

Rosebud Agency

WYOMING

WOUNDED KNEE
MASSACRE

Pine Ridge Agency

NEBRASKA

Niobrara R.

N
W   E
S

North Platte R.

0   Miles   100

There was no use complaining. On each reservation the Indian Bureau chose a number of braves to serve as policemen. The Indian police were paid, drew extra rations, and wore a uniform. Their purpose was not to help the people govern themselves, but to weaken the authority of leaders such as Sitting Bull.

The government also attacked the Indians' religion. A ruling came from Washington abolishing so-called "pagan" ceremonies. For the tribes of the Southwest, this meant an end to the use of mescal, a desert plant whose juices produce visions and dreams. For the plains tribes, it meant an end to the Sun Dance, their holiest ceremony. Beginning in 1885, the army broke up Sun Dance meetings and arrested the dancers.

Meanwhile, in Nevada, a strange thing happened to a medicine man of the Paiute tribe. Wovoka was his name, and he became very ill with a high fever for many days.

While unconscious, Wovoka dreamed that his soul went to heaven and saw God. The Lord told him that the Indians should expect wonderful things to happen to them soon. He, God, would come to earth. He would come from the west, bringing herds of buffalo, deer, and horses to restock the plains. Ahead of Him would roll a wave of fresh earth to cover the spoiled land. The whites would be flung back across the ocean and never allowed to return. Every Indian who ever died would return from the stars to be reunited with their loved ones. Together the Indian peoples would live forever in peace, plenty, and freedom.

But the Indians had to do their part. God, said Wovoka, gave him a new religion to pass on to them. Its commandments were simple: "Do no harm to anyone. Do right always. Do not tell lies. Do not fight. When your friends die, you must not cry."

They must also do a magical dance—the Ghost Dance. Holding hands, the Indians must dance in a circle to the

Wovoka, the Paiute medicine man whose vision began the Ghost Dance religion that swept the western reservations.

An example of an elaborately decorated ghost shirt, which the Indians believed would make them immune to the white man's bullets.

left for four nights once every six weeks. No one need fear the whites, for God had taught Wovoka how to make the ghost shirt, a shirt of white cotton cloth decorated with symbols able to turn away bullets.

The Ghost Dance religion spread throughout the West. It spread because it promised a new, better, world, which was just what the Indians needed. During all of 1889 and 1890, the tribes danced. The circles moved faster, faster, until people fell from exhaustion and dizziness. As they moved, the dancers sang. Each tribe had its own Ghost Dance songs, although the message was always the same:

> My Father, have pity on me!
> I have nothing to eat,
> I am thirsty—
> Everything is gone!

White people living near reservations became frightened. Even though the Indians had been commanded not to fight, they thought the dances were war dances. The braves were dancing to build up their courage, they complained. When the dancing ended, they'd take the warpath and murder every white they could find. Everyone knew the Indians had guns. Some had been hidden when they surrendered, others were bought from greedy merchants, including the latest style Winchester repeating rifles.

The settlers' complaints brought quick results. Again the telegraph wires hummed, bringing eight thousand soldiers to the Dakotas by railroad. General Miles received orders to stop the Ghost Dancing, disarm the Indians, and arrest their leaders until things quieted down.

Ghost Dancers. The Indian with arms outstretched is about to go into a trance during which he hopes to see the spirits of his dead relatives.

Heading the list of those to be arrested was Sitting Bull. Although he had taken part in the dancing, no one has ever proven that he meant to start a Ghost Dance war. Still, Miles couldn't afford to take any chances; for if a war did start, the Hunkpapa leader was sure to join in.

Before dawn, December 15, 1890, Lieutenant Bullhead led forty-three Indian policemen into Sitting Bull's camp. It was a damp, frosty morning, and his men were shivering as much from fear as from the weather.

Lieutenant Bullhead and Sergeants Shave Head and Red Tomahawk barged into Sitting Bull's cabin without knocking. Quickly they woke him from a sound sleep and ordered him to get dressed. Although he did as they said, he was furious at their rudeness.

Like any criminal, he was hustled out of his home between two policemen with a third walking behind. Off to the side he noticed his horse, the one Buffalo Bill had given him, already saddled and waiting.

Word of the arrest had brought hundreds of people to the cabin to see what was happening. Shouts filled the air. Women began to cry. Braves slid cartridges into their rifles.

Just then Sitting Bull came through the cabin door with his guards. He stopped, looked around, and called, "I'm not going! Take action!"

That's all the braves needed to hear. A shot rang out and Lieutenant Bullhead began to fall, dying. As he fell he shot Sitting Bull in the body, while Sergeant Red Tomahawk fired into his back. Sitting Bull pitched forward and lay still.

It was a crazy scene, as Sioux shot at Sioux. In the middle of it all, Sitting Bull's horse took his cue from his act in the Wild West Show. As bullets whizzed overhead, the animal sat down in the middle of the battlefield and raised a hoof as if it wanted to shake hands. The Hunkpapas, thinking their leader's spirit had entered the horse, panicked for a moment.

Their panic allowed the policemen to retreat into the cabin, where they shot Sitting Bull's seventeen-year-old son and held out until rescued by a troop of cavalry.

Sitting Bull's death terrified his people, who began to flee to their relatives on reservations further south. Most were stopped by soldiers and brought back with promises of better treatment.

Only thirty-eight frightened, half-starved people slipped through the soldiers' lines. After traveling a hundred miles, they reached the camp of Chief Big Foot, whose people took them in and shared with them the little food they had.

Big Foot was a Miniconjou Sioux, whose band lived on Pine Ridge Reservation, South Dakota. His name, too, was on General Miles's list of leaders to be arrested. Sitting Bull's people found his camp just as soldiers were closing in from every direction.

Big Foot was glad to see the soldiers. His people were tired of running. The chief himself had pneumonia and was dizzy with fever. A fight was the last thing the Miniconjous wanted.

Big Foot surrendered to Major Samuel Whiteside of the 7th Cavalry, Custer's old regiment. Since the braves were armed, Whitside decided to disarm them next day, after they reached the cavalry base camp and reinforcements. In the meantime, he had the chief placed in an ambulance to make the journey more comfortable.

The cavalry camp was at Wounded Knee Creek. Its commander was Colonel George A. Forsyth, also of the Seventh Cavalry. Forsyth must have thought back fourteen years to the Battle of the Little Bighorn as he watched Big Foot's women setting up their tipis. He and several of his captains had ridden with Major Reno against some of these same Indians.

Forsyth had four hundred seventy cavalrymen to guard

three hundred forty Indians, of whom only one hundred six were warriors. His men ringed the Indian encampment, while four Hotchkiss guns were trained on it from a nearby hill. Hotchkiss guns were small cannon that could fire up to fifty explosive shells a minute.

Next day, December 29, 1890, the colonel ordered his prisoners to hand in their guns. The Sioux held back, fearing they'd be massacred if they disarmed. A few guns were given up, mostly broken ones used by the children as toys.

Forsyth then ordered all the braves to be seated at a council ring near his camp. Big Foot had to be carried from his tipi and placed on the ground near his people. He was weak and couldn't stop coughing.

While cavalrymen watched the braves, others began to search the tipis. Most soldiers treated the Sioux women gently, but a few were on their worst manners that day. They pushed their way into the tipis and began to toss around the Indian's belongings.

Some women were sitting on bundles and refused to stand up when ordered; the bundles had guns hidden inside of them. Soldiers lifted them, screaming, and found the weapons. Thirty rifles turned up.

The braves, meanwhile, were becoming excited as they heard the hubbub from behind. Each man sat with a blanket wrapped around his shoulders. Most had knives under their blankets, some Winchester repeaters.

A medicine man named Yellow Crow walked about, blowing on an eagle bone war whistle and telling them to fight back, since their ghost shirts made them bulletproof.

When the tipi search ended, Forsyth announced that each brave would have to be searched personally. The Indians began to fidget and exchange glances with their eyes. One man opened his blanket, then another. No rifles. Their knives were taken away.

Then it was Black Coyote's turn. He had a Winchester. Waving it over his head, he shouted that it was his. He had paid good money for the gun and intended to keep it. As he brought the gun down, it went off, the bullet flying harmlessly into the air.

We'll never know if Black Coyote meant to harm anyone. For the moment the rifle shot sounded, the other braves threw off their blankets, revealing their guns.

"Look out men, they are going to fire!" a soldier cried.

Both sides blazed away at once at pointblank range. The crack of the rifles mixed with the boom of exploding cannon shells.

Indians shot soldiers. Soldiers shot Indians. Both sides also shot their own people by mistake. Every Indian bullet that missed a soldier plowed into the tipi camp crowded with women and children. Cavalrymen, ringing the braves, shot their comrades on the other side of the circle. When the shooting stopped, Big Foot and at least one hundred fifty Indians, mostly women and children, lay dead. Forsyth's men lost twenty-five killed and thirty-nine wounded, mostly by their own bullets and shell splinters.

Army historians call this tragedy the Battle of Wounded Knee. Indians know it as the Wounded Knee Massacre. But whether a battle or a massacre, Wounded Knee represented two things.

It represented the final scene in the thirty-years' war for the American West. It also meant the end of the Ghost Dance, and with it the Indians' last hope of bringing back the world they knew and loved. The past was gone forever. Soon it would be a fading memory. And the future would be made for them mostly by others.

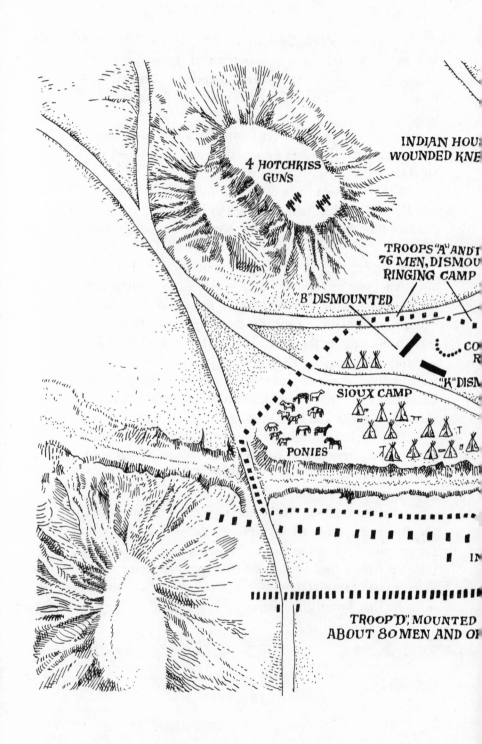

4 HOTCHKISS
GUNS

INDIAN HOU...
WOUNDED KNE...

TROOPS "A" AND "I"
76 MEN, DISMOU...
RINGING CAMP

"B" DISMOUNTED

CO...
R...

"K" DISM...

SIOUX CAMP

PONIES

IN...

TROOP "D", MOUNTED
ABOUT 80 MEN AND OF...

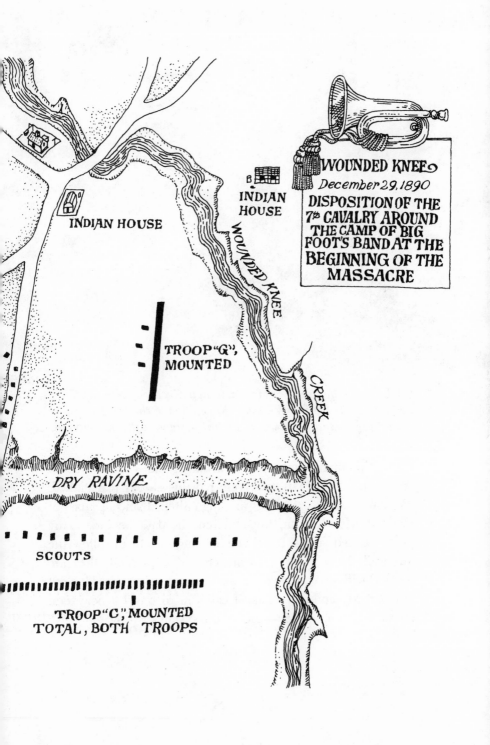

INDIAN HOUSE

B
INDIAN
HOUSE

WOUNDED KNEE

CREEK

WOUNDED KNEE
December 29, 1890
DISPOSITION OF THE
7th CAVALRY AROUND
THE CAMP OF BIG
FOOT'S BAND AT THE
BEGINNING OF THE
MASSACRE

TROOP "G",
MOUNTED

DRY RAVINE

SCOUTS

TROOP "C", MOUNTED
TOTAL, BOTH TROOPS

The body of Chief Big Foot frozen solid in the position in which he died during the fight at Wounded Knee. Men of the Seventh Cavalry, dressed in warm winter uniforms, stand in the background.

One cold, drizzly morning a wrinkled old warrior walked around his camp. His eyes were red, his cheeks tear-stained. As he walked, he called out in a high-pitched voice: "Hoo-oo! Hoo-oo! My children, my children. In days behind, many times I called you to travel the hunting trail or to follow the war trail. Now those trails are choked with sand; they are covered with grass, the young men cannot find them. Hoo-oo! Hoo-oo! My children, today I call you to travel a new trail, the only trail now open—the White's Man's Road."

Some More Books

Ambrose, Stephen E. *Crazy Horse and Custer: The Parallel Lives of Two American Warriors.* Garden City, New York: Doubleday, 1975.

Andrist, Ralph K. *The Long Death: The Last Days of the Plains Indian.* New York: The Macmillan Company, 1964.

Bourke, John G. *On the Border with Crook.* Chicago: Rio Grande Press, 1962.

Brill, C. J. *Conquest of the South Plains.* Oklahoma City: Golden Saga Publishers, 1938.

Brown, Dee. *Bury My Heart at Wounded Knee: An Indian History of the American West.* New York: Holt, Rinehart, and Winston, 1970.

Brown, Mark D. *The Flight of the Nez Percé.* New York: G. P. Putnam's Sons, 1967.

Collier, John. *The Indians of the Americas.* New York: W. W. Norton, 1947.

Custer, George Armstrong. *My Life on the Plains*, ed. M. M. Qualfe. Lincoln, Nebraska: University of Nebraska Press, 1966.

———. *Wild Life on the Plains.* St. Louis, Missouri: The Excelsior Company, 1891.

Debo, Angie. *Geronimo: The Man, His Time, His Place.* Norman, Oklahoma: University of Oklahoma Press, 1977.

Downey, Fairfax. *Indian-Fighting Army.* New York: Scribners, 1941.

Dunn, J. P. *Massacres of the Mountains, 1815–1875.* New York: Archer House, 1958.

Failk, Odie B. *Crimson Desert: Indian Wars of the American Southwest.* New York: Oxford University Press, 1974.

Graham, Colonel W. A. *The Custer Myth: A Source Book of Custeriana.* Harrisburg, Pa.: The Stackpole Company, 1953.

Haley, James L. *Apaches: A History and Culture Portrait.* Garden City, New York: Doubleday, 1981.

Hebard, G. R. *The Bozeman Trail.* Cleveland: Arthur H. Clark, 1922.

Herr, John K. *The Story of the United States Cavalry.* Boston: Little, Brown & Co., 1958.

Hoebel, E. Adamson and Wallace, Ernest. *The Comanches, Lords of the South Plains.* Norman, Oklahoma: University of Oklahoma Press, 1964.

Lowie, Robert H. *Indians of the Plains.* New York: McGraw-Hill, 1954.

Mails, Thomas E. *The Mystic Warriors of the Plains.* Garden City, New York: Doubleday, 1972.

Marquis, Thomas B. *Keep the Last Bullet for Yourself.* New York: Two Continents Publishing Corporation, 1976.

Sandoz, Marie. *The Battle of the Little Bighorn.* Philadelphia: J. B. Lippincott, 1966.

———. *The Buffalo Hunters.* New York: Hastings House, 1954.

Sell, H. B. *Buffalo Bill and the Wild West.* New York: Oxford University Press, 1955.

Tillett, Leslie. *Wind in the Buffalo Grass: The Indian's Account of the Battle of the Little Bighorn River and the Death of their Life on the Plains.* New York: Thomas Y. Crowell, 1971.

Utley, Robert M. *Custer Battlefield National Monument.* Washington, D.C.: National Park Service Historical Handbook, 1969.

———. *Frontier Regulars: The United States Army and the Indian, 1866–1891.* Bloomington, Indiana: Indiana University Press, 1973.

———. *Frontiersmen in Blue: The United States Army and the Indian, 1848–1865.* New York, 1967.

Vestal, Stanley. *Sitting Bull, Champion of the Sioux.* Norman, Oklahoma: University of Oklahoma Press, 1957.

———. *Warpath and Council Fire.* New York: Random House, 1948.

Webb, Walter P. *The Great Plains.* Boston: Ginn & Co., 1931.

Wellman, Paul I. *Death in the Desert.* New York: The Macmillan Company, 1935.

———. *Death on Horseback.* Philadelphia: J. B. Lippincott, 1947.

———. *Death on the Prairie.* New York: The Macmillan Company, 1934.

Index

PICTURE CREDITS